BE POSITIVE
TO
A PLUS

MY TREK THROUGH MDS, AML AND BONE MARROW TRANSPLANT.

MARY GALLO TEICHOLZ

The opinions expressed in this manuscript are solely the opinions of the author and do not represent the opinions or thoughts of the publisher. The author has represented and warranted full ownership and/or legal right to publish all materials in the book.

Forward

AML is a particularly lethal diagnosis, frightening to both patients and doctors alike, especially when it arises from MDS. Thankfully, in my career, seldom have I had to give such grave news and prognosis to patients and family.

Mary Teicholz's story begins with how she discovered, felt and dealt with this threatening diagnosis. She starts out by telling us how the medical system failed her initially with improper communication about her diagnosis, but eventually came through in the end with a life saving medical procedure at a famous Boston teaching hospital.

I found it a warm, funny, informative story with many emotional ups and downs.

What is particularly enlightening about the story is how Mary weaves you through her inner feelings, extracting nuances that I found most interesting. Any patient or family member of any patient going through the process of dealing with a life threatening diagnosis should read this book as it will give you insight into what to ask, expect, and certainly not accept if the health care provider is not giving you the information and support you desperately deserve.

This book also deserves a place on the shelf of any physician in clinical practice.

As physicians we are taught everything we need to know how to get physically better. However, this book gives us the experience of the patient sitting next to us in the examining room. As we all know, as we age and need medical care, eventually we will all be patients, like it or not. It is important that doctors receive the best training to not only provide the best of care, but also the most empathetic care.

Lastly, I would like to comment on Mary's struggle with survivor's guilt. Why did I survive while my friend down the street or across the country did not? As physicians, we are often left with similar lingering doubts when we lose a patient. Why did this person live, and a similar person with the same diagnosis and prognosis ultimately die?

I remember the scene in <u>Saving Private Ryan</u>, at the beginning and end where Tom Hank's character asked the same question. It affected me most dearly. Hopefully we all live our lives so at the end of our lives, the answer is much clearer.

Martin Abrams, MD (a.k.a. Dr Friend)

Be Positive
To
A Plus

By: Mary Teicholz

Introduction

Call me Mary. Call me Mary not only because Ishmael has already been taken, but also because it's my name. The tremendous, overpowering and life-threatening badass beast in my life was blood cancer. Myelodysplastic Syndromes (MDS) related Acute Myelogenous Leukemia (AML) to be exact. The fire in my belly was sheer determination, an unwavering will to survive and a little Italian stubbornness thrown in for good measure. This is my Moby Dick story. This is what happened to me once I reached the shore and realized that I still had a jagged mountain to scale. This is my perception of what has happened in my life because of leukemia and ultimately the need for a bone marrow transplant.

I wanted to tell my story, because while I was going through my battle in the sea and on the land there wasn't anyone I knew that I could relate to. I was dealing with the elements by myself. MDS is a rare disease and honestly, how many people do you know who have had a bone marrow/stem cell transplant?

We are few and far between. Many times I was lonely and I longed for anyone, like myself, to talk to. To tell me they survived. I want people who have to go through these diseases and transplant to know that they aren't alone. I know that not everyone will be able to relate to everything I went through. We all go through our treatment and recovery differently, but I believe that many of the feelings will be familiar.

I'm not ignoring what everyone around me had to go through during my crap storm, but by being in the hospital for months, I just honestly don't know many details. What I do know is that it truly sucked for my family and friends. I do know that sometimes it's harder to watch someone you love fight for his or her life than it is for the person fighting. Well, kind of. I'll be as honest as possible even if it may be a little graphic or off color. My language may not be perfect, but it's how I was feeling at the time. Bear with me.

Chapter 1
Sick and Tired of Being Sick and Tired

It was the end of the summer, 2006 when this all began. I was working at a Holistic doctor's office four days a week and helping a friend campaign for State Representative. My days began at 6:00AM to get my teenage son, Bill, up and out for high school. I would figure out what we would be eating for dinner and I would get myself ready for work. After work, I would be out door knocking, eat dinner and then attend various meetings, sometimes not returning home until ten or eleven at night. At the time, I was also an elected official for the City Council, serving my second term. I was like the energizer bunny. I kept up this pace for months until my right foot began to bother me and I was having a hard time at work keeping my eyes opened after 2:00PM. I distinctly remember someone telling me to "suck it up" when I was tired at a campaign meeting. The guys all kind of laughed and teased me, but they ended up feeling like doo doo in the long run. HA! I also thought that I had bought some really crappy makeup because my blush wouldn't stay on my face and it wasn't giving me a rosy glow. Little did I realize how pale and drawn out I was becoming from my blood being filled with so much craziness! I cut my finger one night while making dinner and it didn't stop bleeding for three days, but I figured I probably should have gotten a couple stitches. And the night sweats…well, what 45 year old woman doesn't wake up sweating at night? I had an excuse for everything, or so I thought.

I woke up one morning and my right foot was bothering me so much that my husband, Lee, convinced me to call my orthopedist. I tried to call my regular ortho, but his appointments were backed up for a couple weeks and I didn't want to wait. I'm a very impatient person at times and this was one of those times. I needed this foot to be fixed NOW!! I had way too many things to do rather than mess around with an injured foot. Ugh, I hate starting with a new doctor, but I was able to get an appointment that day with another area physician. Lee came with me to the appointment and the doctor couldn't find anything wrong. He thought it was all the stress I was putting on my foot from walking up and down the hills while door knocking. I just iced my foot when I was off of it and it still bothered me every morning and loosened up during the day.

Then one morning, a few weeks later, I woke up to both feet hurting and a red line on the side of my right foot below my pinky toe. The doctor I worked for at the time convinced me to go back to the ortho, so I left work early and off I went. This time my ortho doctor did x-rays because he suspected stress fractures. While I was waiting for the results of the x-rays, my cell phone started ringing with calls about campaigning. I hadn't told anyone about my foot/feet except my family, so of course my political friends were wondering where I was on a beautiful day perfect for door knocking. I finally told them I needed a couple days because of my foot, but I would be back very soon. The doctor called me in to his office, he had the results and lo and behold, the x-rays were clean. Crap, crap, crap, what the hell is going on??? No diagnoses, just ice and rest and return to the ortho in a couple weeks if it doesn't get better. Yeah, I didn't rest. I went back to my hectic schedule, pain and all. Like I said before, it did seem to get better as the day went on so I really believed it was overuse.

That was until Thanksgiving morning. Campaigning had been over for a few weeks so there was no reason for the big toe on my right foot to be too swollen to put on regular shoes. I had to wear these ugly, brown, embroidered slipper clogs with a brown velour sweat suit to Thanksgiving dinner at my sister, Mel's friend's house. We had our holiday there because Mel was getting married the next day and her friend was kind enough to have us all over to her home for Thanksgiving dinner. I brought my traditional cornucopia made out of bread surrounded by seasonal fruit and nuts. We were all so excited about the wedding and my sister was so happy. It was truly a time to celebrate. I tried to forget about my stupid foot and prayed that my toe would fit into my shiny bronze heals that matched my brown gown. I was in a brown phase at the time, because I had recently begun coloring my hair red. My hair had been through many changes over the years, so red was just the next color in my arsenal of looks.

The day of the wedding was a wonderful day! My sister and her new husband were beaming and most of our family was together. My foot was killing me, but I wore my heals and changed into ballet slippers to dance. I became very inebriated hoping to lessen the pain. Needless to say, by the end of the night, I felt no pain. This is not something I'm especially proud of, because rumor has it; I wasn't very nice to my other sister, Marlene. I really love both of my sisters and that was a shitty thing for me to do! That actually is the last time I drank alcohol other than a sip here and there. That night, I stayed at the hotel where the wedding took place. Lee and Bill didn't stay over, they decided to head home. While I was taking off my gown, I slipped in the bathroom and hit the backside of my upper arm on the counter. The next morning I woke up with one hell of a hangover and the largest most disgusting black, blue, purple, and green bruise that I've ever seen. It covered a huge portion of my arm. I only showed a few people the bruise and every time the reaction was a gasp quickly followed by an "oh my god." I knew it wasn't normal and I knew my bruising was getting worse. I would bruise even if I would scratch or lean on something. I was just so tired all the time. Again, I made excuses. There was a reason for everything that was happening. On top of everything else, the exhaustion was debilitating. Not a normal tired, a kick your ass, heavy eyelids, can't move your body exhaustion. Things were starting to add up and I think anyone who has a life threatening illness knows on some level, even before diagnosis. Too many things were happening with my body, but I couldn't…wouldn't allow myself to go there.

Okay, so you would think that I rushed right back to the ortho doctor after Thanksgiving, but nooo. I told myself that I was feeling better. Resting my foot was working! NOT! The morning of December 7th I woke up and fell to the floor in pain between the bed and the dresser and just began to cry. Lee came running into the bedroom and made me call the ortho again for an appointment. As usual, my foot felt a little better as the day went on, but I left work for yet another doctor appointment for my stupid foot. Lee met me at the doctor's office and because of the swollen toe this time he wanted blood work, suspecting gout. The ortho asked me if I needed crutches and I said, "yes please." Now if you've ever been on crutches, you know it's not something you practically beg for, but I have to tell you, it was a relief to have crutches. I only used them when the pain was bad, which became most of the time.

When I left the doctor's office, I called my boss and told her what was going on with my foot and I was heading home. I told her I would get the blood work done when I had time. She told me that I needed to go directly to the lab and not wait. I was being a little whiney because I was so tired and sick of going to the doctor. The wonderful physician I worked for basically bullied me into getting the blood work immediately. I think she was connecting the dots and felt like something serious was happening. I went to the lab that day. FYI, I have not stepped foot in that lab since that day. I will go to any other lab, just not there. Even if my husband goes there for his blood work, I wait in the car. That place was the beginning of things that nightmares are made of, the only problem was that I couldn't wake up and make it go away. I was actually living the things I feared the most.

Friday, December 8, 2006, I hobbled to work on my crutches, praying that my lab results would be back and I can go on whatever medication I needed for gout. By the way, isn't gout an old man thing? I had never heard of anyone less than 65 years old getting gout. What the hell! It just figures that I would get something like gout. If only it had been gout. I was beginning to learn that perception is everything. I made the call to Dr Ortho's office later in the morning to ask if my results were back and could they please fax them over to my work. I signed a release and the lab results were sent to me. Within minutes, Dr Ortho called and told me that I needed to send the lab results to my general practitioner, because something was wrong, a serious anemia. He stressed that I had to send the results to my GP immediately! I faxed the lab results right then and there and called the office to tell them that Dr GP needed to look at them ASAP per Dr Ortho. No return call that day and it was Friday so I knew I was screwed. Are you freaking kidding me that I have to wait until Monday! I saw my labs and I had seen enough good labs, working for a doctor, that I knew things really weren't right. There were too many numbers in bold and out of range.

I had shown the results to my boss and my sister's partner, who is a physician's assistant, but neither one, could tell me what they knew. I guess there is a way these things go and it wouldn't have been professional for them to say anything. I spent the better part of that weekend on the Internet desperately, and I really mean desperately, searching for an answer. I kept telling Lee that I didn't think any of this was good. My final analysis was either lupus or leukemia, but what do I know? I could be completely wrong. That's it, I'm completely wrong. I tried to relax and have a good weekend, but I was a little obsessed. What can I do to take my mind off of this nonsense? Christmas shopping! Yeah, that's what I'll do, Christmas shop. Saturday was a good day for my foot, so I was able to head out without my crutches. Yippee, I love Christmas! I decided to shop for Billy, but those pesky thoughts that something was seriously wrong kept creeping into my mind. Oh my gosh, what if this is my last Christmas!!! Well, if it is, I'm going to make this the best one my kid has ever known! I will leave Billy with a wonderful memory. I purchased every item that was on his list and then some. Whatever was going on in my body wasn't going to ruin our Christmas. So there!!!

I know I told my two sisters about my weird blood work and I'm pretty sure I told a couple of my good friends, but other than that, I don't remember. Monday finally arrived and I called Dr GP, but he never returned my call. Jackass! As soon as the doctors' office opened on Tuesday, I was on the phone. The receptionist proceeded to tell me that it was Dr GP's day off, but he might stop in the office. I got off the phone and started to cry. I told Lee what happened and he was pissed. The pressure and anticipation was getting to both of us. This shit had been going on for months. Lee called Dr GP's office and was very forceful in telling them that someone needed to check my blood work…NOW!!!!! I heard the phone slam down.

Chapter 2
The Phone Call
The Beginning

I was sitting on my bed with my crutches leaning against me and I was on the phone with my friend, Kar, telling her about this whole blood work saga, when the caller ID showed Dr GP's number. Finally! I said hello and Dr GP said something like, hi Mary, I checked your blood work and you have leukemia. We need to make an appointment with an oncologist today. My receptionist will make the appointment and call you back. The conversation isn't in quotes, because I think I left my body. My hearing was muffled and I was physically shaking. My first thought was, you no good fucking asshole telling me this over the phone in such a cold manor. I'm fucking freaking out and you are having your receptionist get back to me. What the fuck!!! The first words out of my mouth were yelling for Lee to come upstairs and saying that the jackass Dr GP said that I have leukemia and I need to see an oncologist without delay. I was frantic! Funny, that same idiot doctor delayed my treatment for almost 5 days, which I later realized, could have cost me my life if my leukemia decided to speed up. I called my friend Kar back telling her what was going on, sobbing the whole time. I think she was at my house, sitting on my bed with me within two minutes of the phone call. I was still hoping that this was some kind of mistake. Labs make mistakes. Maybe my blood got mixed up with someone else. This can't be true. I don't want it to be true… I don't want to die!!!

This is the part of the story that is the hardest for me to share so far. I would rather not relive all of it, but something is telling me that I need to do this. I had to take a couple days off from writing, just to wrap my head around what to say next. I still haven't determined if I'm writing this book for me or for other people. Like most things in life, you think you are going in one direction and then you get smacked in the face with something else and the whole thing changes. I'm in this until completion, wherever it may take me or us. Geez, I just don't know. I do know that things get very hazy at this point. Between the shock of hearing I had a life threatening illness and all the medications that are to come, my memories may be slightly jumbled. There are things I honestly don't remember. I suspect it's my minds way of protecting me from all the really, really bad shit. I was also so much in my own head that things people said to me didn't register. The fear of death was too overwhelming!! The fear of everything that was happening was too overwhelming!!!!

Here we go. So, that fucking asshole, Dr GP, actually did have a person in his office call me back with the date and time of my appointment with an oncologist.

I know, I know, I really should let go of my bitterness toward Dr GP, but I don't honestly think I'll ever want to. Anyway, I received the call within an hour of the initial phone call to tell me that I had leukemia. I had stopped crying and I was still holding on to hope that this was some giant mistake. The appointment was scheduled for that afternoon. I was thinking, what is the rush all about? I figured like any other doctor appointment I would have to wait days, if not a week. Crap, this isn't very good if I have to see an oncologist in a couple hours. Lee let his work know that he wouldn't be able to work that night and an eerie quiet fell over my home. There were no words. It was time to shower and get ready for the next life-changing shoe to fall and fall it did! Not just for me, but for my family and friends too. The wrath that occurred for all of us was beyond comprehension.

I heard the shower running and I felt the warm water on my body, but it all sounded and seemed muffled. Like it was happening to someone else and not me. I suppose that is what it would be like to be a zombie; at least I was pale enough to be the living dead. Oh and I was losing weight…okay, that was a positive. I put on my makeup, because for some strange reason I felt the need to look nice as I was heading to the gallows. I'll never forget the sweater I was wearing. It was a turquoise cable knit LL Bean cardigan. I never put it on my back again after that day. I also didn't throw it away. That sweater is up in the attic in a box and I don't know if I ever want to see it again, but I do know that I can't get rid of it. It's kind of funny that it almost feels like an important piece of my life and it's just a sweater. Hmmm?

Lee and I finally headed to the oncologists office that was in the hospital. He dropped me off, due to the fact that I was back on my crutches, and he went to park the car. The ride to the appointment was still that eerie silence. Lee came inside to find me crying outside the double doors that said "Cancer Center." I kept saying very quietly and in between silent sobs, "I don't want to go in there." Number one, I don't have cancer, I might have leukemia, in my mind there was a difference, and number two, if I go in there, it's real. I'm not positive how much time passed before Lee convinced me to walk through those doors, but I remember he said that we are going to be late for the appointment. I really didn't care if I was late. It must have been quite the scene to any onlookers. The poor pathetic 45 year old, on crutches, with her lips quivering and her body shaking afraid to go into the oncologists office. I'm usually pretty tough, but this was a whole different level of frightening.

Chapter 3
Meeting Doctor Friend

As I walked through the doors, I was greeted by a pleasant receptionist named Connie. I would see her very often for the next seven and a half years. I was handed a bunch of papers to fill out and promptly asked my husband to do it for me. I really hate filling all that stuff out. This time my hands were shaking too much and I had no ability to concentrate. We weren't there long before a nurse came out and said my name, probably incorrectly. Everyone mispronounces my last name. I suppose it would be a sad state of affairs if people mispronounced, Mary. HA! We were ushered directly into the doctor's office. Not an examination room, his office. SHIT!!!! I don't know this person; how do I trust him??? This is my life and he was a stranger. Little did I know that there would be many strangers who would have my life in their hands over the next year? How do I know that this guy isn't some kind of hack? It took everything out of me not to bolt.

Dr Friend, my oncologist, looks like a doctor. He is a tall thin man with a relaxed hairline and glasses. I have no recollection of his office, other then Lee sitting to my right and Dr Friend sitting at his desk, facing us. He slowly and methodically began to explain what he saw in the blood work. "Mary, you have leukemia." Acute Myelogenous Leukemia, also known as AML. FUUUUCK!!!! I think he explained more, but I didn't hear anything for a couple minutes. All of my senses had shut off and I became enclosed in a cavernous space where everything seemed so distant. The only thing I heard was Lee sniffing and I was desperately trying to keep it together. Some time passed and I wasn't crying, I was accepting. The first question out of my mouth was, "Can I beat this?" Dr Friend said, "Yes." Next question was, "Will I lose my hair?" Dr Friend said, "Yes." I needed to know exactly how I was going to win this war. I didn't give a crap about my hair; it became so insignificant to me. Dr Friend explained that I needed to have a bone marrow biopsy performed the next day to confirm the diagnosis and to give him more information about the leukemia and blasts and all those medical terms that meant nothing to me at the time, but are a second language to me now. Umm, what is a bone marrow biopsy and isn't that extremely painful? Before any of that nonsense, I needed to go to the hospital lab to have more blood drawn. I was just told that I have leukemia, I'm not even completely positive what that is, and now I'm expected to wait in a dumbass line to have yet another stranger stick a needle in my arm. This is getting to be way too much for me. I wanted to go home and hide. I definitely didn't want to be at the hospital. I made a few phone calls while I waited. I called my two sisters, my friends, Kar and Mon, and the Mayor. Yes, I said the Mayor. I was on the City

Council and he needed to know that I would be out of commission for a while. I may very well have called more people, but who the hell knows. I was in a haze of fire and brimstone.

The gentleman who took my blood was a nice guy. I don't know why, but I told him what was happening with the leukemia stuff. He had huge hands and I wondered if he was going to be gentle at taking my blood especially since I had had a few blood draws in a short amount of time. He did a good job. I didn't feel a thing and he wished me luck with my health as I left. It's funny that I can still picture his hands after all these years. Maybe it was easier to concentrate on his hands instead of what was happening to me. Could it be true that I have leukemia? I need to ask Dr Friend when I see him on Thursday to get my biopsy results. I was so unbelievably tired! I felt like I had been in a prizefight and lost. No prize for me!

This all took place on Tuesday, December 12th so happy freakin holiday to me, to us. The doctor told me not to tell Billy until after the biopsy results. I don't recall his reasoning so I listened and waited two days. Through the conversation with Dr Friend, it came out that I had secretly started smoking again for the past few years. Lee didn't give me hard time about it, he just let me smoke as much as I wanted for the next couple days. I mean, what the hell, I already had cancer. I was prescribed anti-anxiety medication so I could cope and sleep. I was also living on Imodium. Nothing brings on explosive diarrhea like a leukemia diagnosis. We probably should have purchased stock in Charmin. I wasn't especially interested in food, but I tried to keep everything as normal as possible for Bill and Lee. Every time that I started to doze off that night, I gasped in fear. The only way for me to describe it is that feeling you get when you think you are going to fall down the stairs, but you catch yourself and grab your chest. Well it's like that, but the fear doesn't go away because you are free falling. I was terrified of the bone marrow biopsy. I was terrified of having chemo. I was terrified of being sick. I was terrified of dying. I was just terrified! Out of my mind, what the hell did I ever do to deserve being this terrified! It was a very long night.

Wednesday, December 13th was bone marrow biopsy day. I didn't know what to think about the biopsy and I surely had no idea what to expect. This was all new ground for me; leukemia, bone marrow biopsy, and blood counts. What are all these things? This was a world so different from anything I was aware of or anything I ever wanted to know. One of the big fears in my life was cancer. Yikes, I've never shared that before. It was just one of those things, that when people would mention the "c" word, I would feel it in the pit of my stomach. I couldn't imagine ever dealing with it myself, it was way too scary and yet there I was facing this fear. It was becoming my reality. My Mom ultimately died from lung cancer and I will never, as long as I live, forget the fear in her eyes. I remember that cancer has an odor to it and it slowly ravages your body. I remember talking to my Mom about hospice. I remember watching her give in to this terrible disease. This just can't be happening to me. So many thoughts running through my mind, most of which weren't good. Not much praying happening either, I was pissed. I was thinking why was God letting this happen to me? Then I thought, why not?

Biopsy day was upon me. I got a little sidetracked, but that was my state of mind at the time. Lee and I were heading back to hospital, which would become our home away from home for the next six weeks. We were told to wait in the same chairs where we had waited the day before to have additional blood taken. Those stupid ugly floral upholstered chairs. Germ infested yucky chairs. The place was packed and peoples' voices were getting on my nerves. Why don't these people shut the hell up? Don't they realize that my body is turning on me? Please just shut up with all your nonsense!! Shut up! Shut up! Shut up! Finally, they called my name. Finally, some relief from all the inane conversations going on all around me. Oops, I needed to hit the bathroom first. I already told you what happens to my digestive system when I'm nervous. It's not a pretty sight. I can't believe that I actually crapped in so many public places and so often. I hate public bathrooms.

Chapter 4
The Biopsy

So Lee and I were ushered into what would be the first of many examination rooms. The exam table was pushed up against the wall and there was a chair, not upholstered, in the corner for Lee to sit on. It was a larger than average room. Probably because of the Frankenstein like procedure they were about to perform on my body. I was scared, very scared. Lee looked a little pale also. It was so much to take in, in a very short time. In walked a lovely young Indian woman with long dark hair. She was wearing the typical doctor uniform, but she was a resident. She was my preliminary doctor, if there is such a thing and she asked me a ton of questions. Then, the resident began to explain the biopsy procedure to us in detail. Depending on the doctor, you either lay on your side or your stomach. I think I was on my side for the first biopsy. Yes, first biopsy, there were many more to come in the following year. Needles are systematically put into your hip, numbing each layer of muscle as the Dr. proceeds until the hipbone is reached. At that point the biopsy is retrieved/aspirated from the bone. I was shaking in my friggin boots. No, I really was shaking. The resident said she would stay with me through the whole thing and she would hold my hand, which she did. Thank goodness for her. I wish I knew her name; she was awesome. She was trying to mentally prepare me for what was going to happen.

Soon after, the doctor who was going to perform the biopsy entered the room. He was an African American gentleman and he spoke to me gently. He's obviously done this before. Okay, please let's get going already! The anticipation is killing me faster than the damn leukemia! The first needle enters my hip. It's not too bad. Many more needles enter my hip and I think I said ouch quite a few times, but the pain wasn't terrible. Finally we were at the hipbone so no more little needles. Oh no, out came the big guns. Mind you, I can't see any of this, but my husband saw the whole thing. The doctor needed to take a small chip off of the bone and punctured the bone with another needle in order to aspirate the marrow. I would say that it was more pressure than pain at this point. You have to be one strong mother to puncture into a huge bone like a hipbone. Once the specimens are retrieved, the biopsy is finished. Now, I absolutely realize that it sounds scary as hell and painful, but it wasn't terrible. The very worse part of the whole thing was not knowing how it would feel, how much pain there would be, how it would feel afterwards and of course what the results would tell us. Anticipation and fear were the worse part of this whole damn thing. The aftermath felt like a bruise for a couple days. All I had to do is position myself on one side of my hiney when I sat down and keep the butterfly bandage for a short time. That's it! The entire biopsy took about 20-30 minutes. I was emotionally wrecked! I needed to prepare myself for the next day, which was another day of results and worry. I needed a cigarette.

December 14th of 2006 was a Thursday. Another day of going to the doctor and seeing that blasted "Cancer Center" sign, but what else was new! I was keeping in touch with my boss through all of this and she was very supportive. I hadn't been to work in a week. Like I said, she is a holistic doctor and also a licensed physician. She really knew what was happening, even better than I did. She knew that I would never be able to return to my job. I didn't know that though. I figured I would get through whatever treatment was in store for me and then everything would be back to normal. Yup, I was delusional. My life was on the verge of changing forever and I had no idea. All I knew was that this shit was getting very old very quickly.

Lee and I were back in front of that ominous "Cancer Center" sign for the second time in a few days. It still caused me to pause before entering the office. Okay, here we go. I was going to hear that it was all a big mix up and all I had was a virus. Write me a prescription and I'm out of here! Of course, that wasn't what happened. Dr Friend told us that the diagnosis of AML was confirmed through the bone marrow biopsy. I didn't honestly have to be told that, because I already knew. I had known it on some level since the first time I saw my blood work. What do we do now? Dr. Friend explained that I would have to be admitted into the hospital for approximately a month. Wait, did I hear that right......A MONTH!! NO, NO, NO!!! It's Christmas time! Just NO! I wasn't taking that news very well. I asked Dr Friend if there was any way that I could hold off until after Christmas. He said on one condition; that I go to his office every morning and have my blood drawn. If there is any change in my labs, I will be admitted to the hospital immediately. He explained that AML could go very bad very quickly. I understood and agreed with these conditions. I also had to get some baseline testing done. I had lung x-rays and a stress test to make sure my heart and lungs were strong enough to handle the treatment. At the time, I didn't realize that this meant that I was getting some really strong shit (chemo) that people don't always survive if they have other underlying health conditions. Ignorance was bliss in this case.

Chapter 5
Telling Bill

That evening, my husband and I decided that it was time for me to tell our son what was happening. How the hell do you say this to your kid! Holy shit, I needed to do this right. You see, my Dad died from heart disease right when I turned seventeen. I entered my senior year of high school without a father. History better NOT be repeating itself!! I grew up with a sick parent, so I knew better than anyone else what a giant crap sandwich this was going to be for Bill. I remember my dad being in the hospital for a month at a time. I remember missing him and feeling very much in the dark. I remember everyone tip toeing around me, because I was the baby of the family. I remember the pain of losing a parent, but being so concerned with how my mother was doing, that I kept it all inside. I remember the kids at school whispering when they saw me and saying to each other, did you hear that her father just died? I remember that I missed the appointment for my senior picture because I was at my father's funeral. They called to see why I missed the appointment during the funeral party. Sorry, but that's what I call it. "Umm, my dad died and I'm at the funeral party now." I remember the loneliness. I was THAT kid and I didn't want my son to have to endure the same thing.

So the time came to ask Bill to please come up to the bedroom we needed to talk to him. Honestly, I did all the talking. I said, "So, you know about my foot and how I've been going for all kinds of tests. Well, they found something called leukemia." I didn't want to say cancer. I told him it was AML and they caught it early, before I was extremely sick. That was kind of true. I think I eventually did say that it was a blood cancer and that I would be in the hospital for about a month and the doctor said I could beat it. I explained that I would be going for blood work every morning etc.. I was as honest with him as I was able to be at the time. My family had left me in the dark when my dad was sick and I was shocked when he passed away. How do you prepare your child and not scare the heck out of them at the same time? I'm not sure I did the best job at achieving that balance. Lee was standing behind Billy during the conversation and tears were flowing down his face. Bill was very calm and I asked him if he had any questions and I let him know I would answer to the best of my ability. I don't recall any questions, but I do suspect that he went right to the Internet. That whole conversation goes down in history as one of the most terrible conversations of my life. I didn't know what was going on in Bill's head. It was heartbreaking. That night, I smoked a cigarette, and then I threw the rest of the pack away. No more cigarettes for me, ever!

Life was quiet until Saturday. My husband went to the dry cleaner and someone from the hospital recognized him and told him to make sure that I get a second opinion. This person was insistent. We listened. I have friends who have a family member who is a very specialized oncologist in New York City. That's who I called and I was able to get an appointment with a Park Ave. oncology hematologist, Dr P, for Monday afternoon. My friends and their family member definitely helped me out when I had no idea where to turn. Lee and I decided that things were getting very serious so we gave Bill his big Christmas present, an X Box, on Saturday. I wasn't sure that I would be home for Christmas with the way things were going and I needed to see my son get excited about something. We also thought it would help keep his mind off of all the crap going on around him. Wouldn't you know the damn friggin thing broke and we had to send it back? So now I had to tell him that I didn't think we would be able to get a new one before Christmas, but lo and behold the new one showed up on Christmas Eve!

Monday morning I went to get my blood drawn and I saw Dr Friend. I told him that I wanted a second opinion and he said absolutely. He gave me a copy of my biopsy results and a few other papers to bring with me to my appointment. I kept looking at the comment at the end of my biopsy results, but I didn't know what it meant. It was bugging the crap out of me. I knew something wasn't right. What does myelodysplasia related leukemia mean? I thought it may have been just one of those doctor talky things. Maybe it had already been explained to me and I didn't absorb the information. I was too afraid to ask too many questions, because I couldn't handle any more bad news, my mind was shutting down.

Lee was so good at pushing me to see any and all doctors immediately, even if it meant we were driving all over the place to see them. In retrospect, I realize how hard this was for him, but at the time, I only wanted to figure this shit out and be healthy. I really wanted someone to tell me that the Connecticut doctors were wrong and some strong antibiotics would take care of everything. I already had wicked diarrhea so my stomach wouldn't feel much worse with some strong meds. Instant diet, just be told you have the "c" word and your appetite flies right out the window and everything else flies out your butt. How much worse can chemo really be? Answer is: quite a bit.

Chapter 6
NYC

So we get to the city, fyi; Lee hates driving in the city, and there is no place to park. Shocking, in NYC and can't find a parking space? Ugh! Lee dropped me off in front of this building on Park Ave. and I hobble in on my crutches. There was a nice doorman, who helped me up a few stairs and led me to the doctor's office. I told him that my husband was parking the car and he said he would bring him to me. I couldn't believe I was in a very ritzy part of NYC and a doorman was helping me. Surreal! But what wasn't surreal about the last week or so. Every step was an out of body experience. Occasionally, I would cry and ask Lee if I was going to live through this. I knew he didn't know any better than I did, I just needed to hear a yes, you will be fine. The anti-anxiety meds also helped. Thank goodness for that stuff! Well that and anti-diarrhea medicine.

Dr P's waiting room was small and we were the only people in there. I suspect that I was fit in as the last patient as a favor to her colleague. I was extremely grateful for the appointment. Here we go, another doctor's examination room. In walks Dr P, an attractive young woman with shoulder length dark hair. She made me comfortable immediately. She wanted to take some blood for the second time in one day. I have to admit that my veins were really starting to hurt. It was getting quite painful to constantly have blood taken and to have low platelets. Platelets clot your blood, so I looked like a bruised mess. I took a deep breath and said okay. She was looking over my paperwork and saw that comment that I was worried about. My intuition was correct. There was more to worry about, as if I wasn't freaking out enough.

I also had MDS (myleodysplastic syndromes). It was classified as a group of blood disorders or pre-leukemia or smoldering leukemia, but is now sometimes considered a cancer. FUUUCK! That's what I was yelling in my head. Oh and it's considered a rare disorder. Of course it is!!! Are you fucking kidding me? Oh and you may need a bone marrow transplant. A WHAT! What the fuck is that? I really wanted to say, "Now, you are just messing with me, right?" If I were an artist, I would draw a picture of my head freaking exploding all over the doctor and the exam room. Okay, I really was living an episode of the Twilight Zone. Dr P wanted me to see another physician at a New York City hospital who does bone marrow transplants. She gave me his information and I was to call him the next day. Lee and I left the city that was shimmering with Christmas lights and huge snowflakes on the buildings and most people were feeling the magic in air. I was feeling desperation. I was feeling hopeless. I was feeling like I would never feel normal again. I was scared out of my mind!

The sequences of events are sketchy for the next week or so. I do recall going to the NYC hospital. Again, parking was difficult so Lee dropped me off with my crutches. Lovely, here I am on a New York City street alone and on crutches and filled with the "c" word. As you might be able to tell, I still, all these years later don't like saying or typing the word …cancer. I'll stick to "c" word. It's also lower case to diminish the power of the "c". It doesn't deserve to be capitalized. I made it inside to a giant waiting room and I mean giant. I don't know how many chairs there were, maybe three hundred, or that's what it looked like and they were all filled up with people. A nice young man got up from his seat and offered it to me. I think the crutches did it and I was grateful. Lee was parking the car forever, while I was filling out all the paperwork for yet another doctor. I hated being there. There were lots of germs around me and I was extremely susceptible to infections. Oops, I forgot that while I was going through all the foot bullshit, I also developed walking pneumonia and bronchitis. I guess I really was displaying many symptoms. It's funny how many important things about this experience, I've forgotten and how many insignificant things I remember.

The next doctor in what seemed like the never-ending line of doctors was Dr L. I had more blood taken out of my arm, which was getting more painful with every stick of a needle. I was getting aggravated. Dr L actually brought me into an examination room on the bone marrow floor and talked to me about my lab results. He had seen the bone marrow biopsy results and agreed with Dr P that I had AML brought on by MDS. Heavy sigh! The big problem with the MDS portion was that it makes it harder to treat the AML and even if they are able to get me into remission, the MDS will bring me out of remission quickly. This type of AML comes back with a vengeance, making it more difficult to treat. Dr L said I needed to give a lot more blood (it felt like a gallon) to send out to have my information put into the National Bone Marrow Registry to try to find a bone marrow match. The best thing would be to have a sibling match, but there was only a thirty percent chance of one of my two sisters being my match. I was listening to the doctor and taking it all in while my brain was yelling many obscenities. I was in shock. Maybe this thing was going to be way more difficult then I originally thought it would be. I kept grabbing Lee's hand and I kept asking him to please get me out of there. While I was in the lab area waiting for them to take that gallon of blood, I started crying. The room wasn't as clean as I was used to. The thought again of germs was upsetting me and the shear magnitude of what I just heard was making me loose hope. If I could have run away, I would have. I wanted to escape.

I saw Dr P on Park Ave. again that week and it was all the same stuff I had already heard. Both physicians had been in constant contact with Dr Friend and they were all on the same page. The first step was to have both of my sisters tested to see if either one of them were my bone marrow match. Dr Friend asked me a series of questions about my sisters and their health. He explained to us that you don't need to have the same blood type to be a matched donor, as a matter of fact my blood type would change to the donors blood type. That blew my mind. My blood type would change? Not just that, but if my donor was a male, my chromosomes would become XY instead of XX. Would I even be myself anymore? In the midst of this conversation, I chimed in asking if I would become a lesbian like my sister Marlene if she were my match? And then I joked about being the only Republican in the family. You need to understand that in my family, teasing each other is a way of life. You better have a thick skin if you want to join in our ranks. Marlene is extremely good-natured and gives it right back to me. The family rags on me for my political party affiliation, for dating many guys named Steve and only marrying Jewish men. None of the teasing is mean spirited. We all love and respect each other just the way we are. I knew, without a doubt, that both of my sisters would step up and get tested to see if they were my bone marrow matches. Amazingly enough, I have heard quite a few stories about siblings who wouldn't get tested at all, even some that were tested and found to be a match and then they backed out. I'm very lucky to have the sisters I have, neither one of them hesitated when I asked them to be tested.

My sister, Marlene is the oldest. She has an extremely good sense of humor and would give you the shirt off of her back in a second, if you asked for it. Melanie, my middle sister, is more intense. We tease her about not liking people, but that isn't true. Many of her friends are the same friends that she had in high school. We all look very similar and there is no doubt when anyone sees us together, that we are sisters. We are also very different from each other. All of our personalities are diametrically opposed to each other. Sometimes we all piss each other off and sometimes we don't understand where the other one is coming from, but no one better mess with us. The greatest thing about us is that we are a team. We've always had each other's backs. We love each other and I knew this nonsense was going to be a group battle.

Chapter 7
Christmas Time

The next step in this saga was to begin induction therapy, the chemo to attempt to get me in remission, right after Christmas. Dr Friend wanted me in the hospital on December 26th, but I begged for one more day. I didn't want to spend, what I feared was my last Christmas, worrying about the next day. Although he wasn't very happy about it he reluctantly agreed to give me one more day. There was at least one doctor appointment every day until Christmas Eve. Most of them consisted of paperwork and me asking Lee to get me out of wherever I was. The only times I felt calm were when we went for rides to see Christmas lights and when I went to my friend Kar's house to watch the deer in her backyard. The deer came out about four o'clock every day and for some reason, I loved watching them. The deer would cautiously emerge from the woods behind Kars house to have their evening snack. I may have been relating to them. Those cute deer knew they were being watched and hunted. Just like the "c" word was hunting me down to kill me. I would watch them nibbling on the food and then disappear back into the woods. I wished that I could have disappeared.

There is something that anyone who knows me, knows how much I love to bake and as you can imagine, Christmas time is the Olympics of baking. Baking is how I relax. Baking is my artistic outlet. Normally, I would have been making cookies for weeks, but not in 2006. Between all the doctors appointments and the crutches, no goodies came out of my kitchen that year. The holiday cookies are normally a yummy family history. I always make my Nonni's stufoli, which are little fried dough balls covered in warm honey and nonpareils. I like to make them on a Saturday morning. I'm not sure why, it's just become my tradition. I make chocolate crinkles and that recipe came from my neighbor, Mrs. H, who lived across the street from me while I was growing up. I still have the recipe in her handwriting and she was very special to me. Spritz cookies are the only cookies that Billy would help me make when he was young. Well, I would make them and he would decorate them with lots of different sprinkles and red-hot candies. The kitchen floor also ended up being decorated with sprinkles. The recipe for peanut butter blossoms came from my sister-in-law, Carol. She is one of Lee's sisters and she passed away suddenly in January 2015, so you see why the cookies are a family history. There are other cookies that have rotated in and out over the years, but these are the staples. There are many memories in those cookies, but not that year.

Christmas Eve is a very big deal in an Italian family and that is the one holiday meal that I host every year.

The main menu doesn't vary from year to year. Appetizers consist of a vegetable platter made to look like Santa, dip and something called veggie bars. Santa's beard is made of cauliflower, his hat is made of red peppers, his nose is a cherry tomato, his smile is also a red pepper and his eyes are slices of radishes with olives cut in half. My sister, Melanie, thinks it's funny to eat his eyes every year and then deny doing it. We tease about Santa's eyes and somehow, it's always funny. The main part of the meal is chicken and shrimp, cooked in a port wine sauce over linguine, an antipasto salad and homemade garlic bread. I know, I know, it's not the true Italian seven fishes, but it's what we like and the chicken and shrimp recipe was something my mother loved. Guess what dessert is…cookies and a store bought cheesecake. None of this is what happened that fateful Christmas Eve.

I cried to Lee at the thought of not having Christmas Eve at our house. I needed to have it in our home. I felt a sense of desperation. Lee went out and bought all the food at our local grocery store. We had trays of cheeses, and cold cuts and vegetables and anything else he thought would be yummy. We set the table for a buffet, I normally hate buffets for holidays, but this was different. I decorated with crystal bowls filled with ornaments and a red tablecloth. Everything looked festive. Festive is important to me. I'm that person who changes her kitchen curtains, shower curtain, towels, bedding and every inch of our home is decked out in Christmas décor. Even that Christmas, but I have no idea how I did the decorating or when I had the energy. The best surprise of the day was that Bill's new Xbox 360 came in and he was very excited when he opened the box. Surprisingly enough, it ended up being a very nice holiday filled with laughter, family, friends and love. For a couple days, there were no hospitals or doctors and the "c" word didn't exist. Lee did an incredible job at putting together a great Christmas Eve!

December 26th was a contemplative day. I straightened up the house and packed for my month long hospital visit. I knew it was going to consist of chemotherapy for seven days and I would feel like I had a terrible flu. That was all I really knew. It could be that that was all my brain wanted me to know. I was embracing the thought of being bald and I wondered about my true hair color. I had been coloring my hair for so long, it was a mystery. My first gray hair appeared when I was thirteen, so chances were I would have salt and pepper locks. I wondered how sick I was going to be and if I would be throwing up all the time. I despise throwing up. I was worried about Lee and Billy and how they were going to handle this whole thing.

Chapter 8
The Council

I can't remember exactly what day it was in those last few days before the hospital, but I do remember going to city hall to say goodbye to everyone. I was asked if they should keep my illness quiet and I said no. The way I looked at it was, it was going to be obvious that something was wrong with me and I would rather people heard the truth, so they didn't make shit up. I know that there were people who thought I was going to be pushing up daisies. The mayor, some members of his staff and various other city employees hung out in the reception area of the mayor's office with Lee and I for about an hour. The reception area has a couple chairs and a small sofa, a coffee table, a Christmas tree and the receptionist's desk. Everyone kind of gave me the sad head tilt when they saw me. Other people just welled up with tears. I said over and over again, in a cheerful voice that I would see them in a month. They didn't believe me. I told them that I was going to be at the February City Council meeting. I could almost hear them saying, "yeah, right." The final stop in city hall was the council chambers. It was dark when Lee and I entered the room so I walked over to the lights and turned the ones on over the dais. The twenty-one-seat dais can be intimidating to look at from the audience, but for me it was home. I walked up the two stairs to my seat.   I sat down, leaned forward to touch my nameplate and began to sob. I rested my head in my arms and cried like a baby. I asked Lee if I would ever really sit in my seat again. He said yes, but I saw the tears in his eyes. We were as unsure as everyone else.

Three years earlier, I had won my first election. I'll never forget the day the mayor asked me to run on his ticket. We were at a Fourth of July picnic and he came over to me and asked if I would be interested in running for office. My response was one word, "sure." In my head I was so excited, because I had been trying for years to run for the City Council, which was actually called the Common Council at the time. I had interned at our State Capitol when I was in college, this politics stuff was in my blood. Oh wait, leukemia was in my blood. Politics was something that intrigued me. Putting my first yard sign up with my name on it was something I wish my Mom and Dad had lived to see. I was so afraid of losing. All the candidates worked hard that year and because so many of us were new, we also built some amazing bonds. Election day came and seeing my name on a ballot was surreal. It took me forever in the voting booth, because I kept staring at my name. I couldn't believe that people would actually vote for me! My nerves were shot by the time the election results came in. When we heard that I won, I hugged my family and jumped up and down and I was ready to celebrate. Little did I know what was to come in a few years.

Chapter 9
First Chemo

December 27th came quickly and slowly all at once. I brought the biggest suitcase we owned, filled with jammies, underwear, socks, pictures, toiletries, and some street clothes. I wasn't sure what to bring for a month long visit to the hospital; I mean who the heck spends a scheduled month in a hospital. I purchased an electric razor for my legs, because you can't use regular razors when your platelets are low, unless you want to bleed to death. I also brought my stepper and sneakers to exercise as long as the doctor allowed it and slippers because I wasn't allowed to be bare foot. I honestly tried to figure out how to look cute through this process. That was short lived. Kind of hard to look cute when you feel like dookey.

I opted not to bring my crutches to the hospital with me. I walked in on my own. I don't know why I needed to do that; I only knew that it was necessary. I had to go to a part of the hospital that I wasn't familiar with to have a picc line put into the underside of my arm. It's a minor procedure, but I was so afraid and angry every step of the way. All I knew at this point was that the chemo goes into that line and I wasn't going to be stuck with any more needles as long as that was in my arm. I remember still being in my street clothes when they brought my up to the oncology floor. I was screaming in my head that I wanted to go home. The nurse led me to a room with two beds. Hold on a minute!! I'm supposed to have a private room and who is this stranger in the other bed. Get me the hell out of here!!!! NOW! Leukemia patients get their own rooms, because we are there for so long and because of germs. Why am I in this room? As if I wasn't frightened enough, they were messing with the agreement that I wouldn't be sharing a room. I didn't want to be around sick, maybe dying, people. The room was dark and icky and the person in the next bed was moaning. Fuck you all! The inside of my head had a lot of bad language. A few bad words may have flown out of my mouth along the way.

Lee needed to leave and the sheer magnitude of my fear was indescribable. The nurse told me that they were starting chemo immediately and they were working on the private room. I was wearing my short sleeve light blue henley shirt, jeans and sneakers. I never wore that shirt again either. I think it's in the box in the attic with the turquoise cable sweater. Maury Povich was on the TV doing more of those ridiculous paternity tests. This woman was having the 20th man tested to see if he was the baby daddy. I wanted to just watch TV so I could distract myself from reality. I didn't want to be sick. Please God make this all go away. I was desperate for all of this to go away. I was angry that this was happening to me. It's not fair! My nurse was about to connect the bag of chemo and my body was shaking with fear. I was seriously shaking and chaos had taken up residence in my head! Then she told me that she needed to piggy back another chemo. Meaning a second chemo was pushed into the first line of chemo. Holy craparooie, I don't want to be barfing for a month. Please stop, PLEASE! I was fighting back the tears. I chose to escape and decided to watch the TV. The nurse and I were talking about the woman with all the paternity tests and out loud I said, "Wow, what a slut!" We both started laughing. Some of the tension inside of me began to dissipate. At that moment, I realized that laughter would help me navigate through this new world. Joking about this illness became a way of life. I had two choices, I could be miserable and negative or I could make the best of it, either way I had to go through it. I chose humor, which wasn't always easy. I chose to be as positive as possible.

The fear of having leukemia and all the other nonsense was extremely overpowering. Not knowing what the chemo was going to do to my body and throwing up and losing my hair and who the hell knew what else was coming my way was an awful lot to handle. I was mad at God. I didn't understand why I was chosen to go through this. I still haven't figured that part out, but I'm usually not as pissed as I was in the beginning. I do have my moments of annoyance though. I imagine the "why me" will always be a small part of my psyche. I don't dwell on it, but it's there. The real, big time fear was my mortality. The fear of dying can't be put into words. It's introspective. Unlike the fear of treatment when people could tell me what to expect from chemo, no one can tell you what to expect from death. It's all faith based and I wasn't too keen on the whole faith thing at this point. I was shaken to my core and completely confused. I was raised Catholic and went to Catholic schools for twelve years. I had a strong faith and I needed to reevaluate what I had believed since I was a young girl. I believed in heaven and the Holy Trinity and all the things I had been taught, but this new endeavor made me pause. If I died, where would I go? I wasn't positive any more. If there was a heaven was I really a good enough person to go there? I relived many of the crappy things I had done in my life and I hoped I wasn't too shitty. I hoped that I had done a ton more good things in my life than bad, but I'm not the judge. What would it be like? St. Peter at the pearly gates passing judgment? A beautiful field with all my loved ones who had gone before me there to greet me? A place to right all of my wrongs? I wondered what my Mom and Dad went through when they realized they were dying. Were they as frightened as I was or did they come to terms with it somehow? I didn't know and I didn't want to talk about it to anyone. The whole thing was way too real for me. My body was dying at this point and I knew it. I was scared to death. Maybe that was a bad chose of words, I was very scared.

By the time the nurse had finished piggy backing the chemo, my private room was ready. If the hospital had been a hotel, my room would have been the penthouse suite. It was the nicest hospital room that I had ever seen. When you opened the door to my room, there was a small hallway with the bathroom to the right. The room was a corner room with tons of windows and light, which I liked. There were built in wood cabinets for me to keep all of the essentials. My bed was in the center of the room facing one set of windows and the other set was to my right with a chair right next to the bed. There was another reclining chair on the other side where Lee liked to take his naps and two additional chairs facing the bed for visitors. There are two of these rooms on the oncology floor for the long-term patients. The other room had a shower, but mine didn't. My shower was up the hall and I really hated going in there. Anyway, my room was awesome. I filled the ledges with pictures of my family and animals. There were also lots of goodies in my room for guests and nurses. I had piles of magazines that I would sit in the chair and read. It became my home for a little while. Well, I say a little while, but it felt like an eternity.

Chapter 10
Settling In

Day two was interesting. I still had on my blue Henley shirt because the picc line was in my arm and I had to wait for the chemo bag to finish. Then I could be unhooked and get cleaned up and changed. For one solid week I received chemo 24 hours a day. I went from one chemo bag right into the next. UGH!! On this day, everyone and their brother came to visit me. I think they all wanted to get the visit in before I got really sick and they wouldn't know what to say to me. It was nice. All the mucky mucks in city government and some from the state came to visit that day. After everyone left, an aide came into my room and said, "Was that just the mayor in your room? Who the hell are you?" I laughed and said "nobody." Titles were inconsequential at this point. People would tease me and say, "Who the heck do you know to get this room?" I kept telling everyone that it wasn't who I knew, it was what I had wrong with me that got me this sweet room. I would have loved to be anywhere other than where I was. I spent a lot of time imagining that I was anywhere other than where I really was.

That evening a nurse came into my room to change my chemo bag, take my vitals and let me get cleaned up and changed finally. I opted to wear the hospital johnny coat, because it was easiest with the picc line. The snaps at the shoulder made it easier for me to change more often and less laundry for Lee. After we finished getting me all together, the nurse, I wish I could remember her name, went to hang my new chemo bag and said, "Here is your liquid gold. It's making you better!" Wait!!! What did you just say to me? Holy shit, she was right. I was looking at this thing completely wrong. Okay, so I know chemo is poison and sucks, but it was ultimately going to make me better! I needed to embrace this stuff and not be so freaked out by it. That was the moment that I learned about perspective. The thing I feared was also the thing that was going to heal me. WOW! A light bulb went off in my head. I was looking at everything in a whole new light. Go team Mary!

I decided that this hospital garb was a little too boring for me, so I jazzed it up with various color ties around my waist. First of all the belts kept my ass from peaking out of the back of the gown and second of all, I was developing a new hospital fashion statement. My two favorite tie/belts were a furry green one that I could also use as a neck warmer and a bright pink very thick ribbon. On occasion I would wear the light blue or the multicolor ties that I had purchased in Mexico. They needed to be tied tighter and tighter as the month in the hospital progressed. The yucky white hospital gown with the blue design was my new uniform. I also opted not to shave my head like many other "c" word patients do. I'm not judging, we just all have different ways of going through this stuff. I did have it cut above my shoulders that first week. My hair had been down my back since college, so my friends were all curious to see me with short hair. I'm glad I made that decision because I lost most of my hair from my crown at first. I was able to wear hats to cover the hair loss until I went into transplant. I still had my bangs and the back of my hair. It was weird.

A couple days after I had begun my chemo, my arm with the picc line started to swell. At first they thought that I had developed a DVT or deep vein thrombosis. Someone told me, I can't recall if it was the nurse or a doctor that if the swelling didn't go down, they would have to stop chemo and take out the picc line. Stop my chemo!!!! Are you all out of your freaking minds? I just got used to the thought of this crap coursing through my veins and now you want to stop it!! I was sitting in the windowsill in my room sobbing when two of the attorneys from city hall came to visit. I got a hug and told them what was happening, but I was pissed that they saw me being so weak. Only my very close friends and family had ever witnessed me letting my guard down. Oh, and my doctor and nurses, but it was rare. How things change! A few days prior, I was shaking at the thought of chemo and suddenly I was afraid of not getting my chemo. What a roller coaster ride of emotions! The doctor decided to wrap my arm in ice and we would see how it was the next day. I had to lie in bed with ice blankets surrounding my arm. It was cold and very difficult to sleep. The next morning my arm was unwrapped and all was well. PHEW! Finally, something went my way. So the chemo continued. The funny thing is, is that my right arm still swells to this day. I don't know if it is related or not, but it always reminds of the night I wanted my chemo.

Chapter 11
New Years Eve and On

I actually had fun on New Years Eve in the hospital. Bill insisted that him and Lee spend the night in the hospital with me. They came up and brought pizza, a cheese and cracker platter and soda. I had stopped eating a couple days earlier and the smell of the pizza was kind of gross, but I was so happy they were there. Bill and I played tic tac toe with a political set a friend had given me. Instead of X's and O's the pieces were donkeys and elephants. We were all chatting about what was going on with me and suddenly Bill started explaining what platelets were and the different blood cells. That is when I realized that he was looking stuff up on the Internet. The only thing I could do was reiterate that he could come to me with any questions and if I couldn't answer them, I would ask my doctor. For the rest of the night we all laughed and joked around and watched the ball drop together at midnight. I was very touched that my teenage son wanted to be with me on New Years Eve instead of with his friends. I've always wondered what Lee and Billy were experiencing during this crap storm. Neither one of them ever said very much.

The big problem with getting chemo twenty-four hours a day, other than getting chemo twenty-four hours a day, was having to unplug the IV machine any time I needed to move around the room. I think anyone who has had massive amount of chemo knows that you need to spend quite a bit of time in the bathroom. I wasn't a thrower upper, I was the diarrhea girl. Not only that, but all of my pee and poop had to be monitored. So friggin disgusting! The routine went something like this. Step one, was to get my exhausted butt out of bed. Step two, lean over and unplug the IV. Step three; walk around my bed and down the small hallway to the very large bathroom with my new appendage. Step four; poop, poop and poop some more. At one point an infectious disease doctor was called in because they thought that I might have c-dif, which is a very bad infection, but I didn't. Step five; get cleaned up from the messy process. And repeat. It never ended! Finally, I would make the trek back to bed. Occasionally, I would forget to plug the machine back in and when the battery would get low there would be a very annoying beeping. Just like the beep when my IV bag was empty or the stupid machine was being ornery or the line would get a kink. I swear that thing woke me up all the time. It took a few days to get used to being hooked up to something and never being without it. By the way, the hospital is definitely not a place to get sleep and relax. It's worse than having a newborn. Just sayin'.

My days usually began with none other then a trip to the bathroom. On my way there, I would stop by my laptop and turn it on. There was only dial up, so I knew that by the time I was finished with my morning constitution, I would be able to post to my CarePages and check email or Internet shop. I tried to get this in before Dr Friend would come to check on me. He usually showed up about 6:30AM and he had a very distinctive walk. I could always tell when he was heading toward my room, because I was at the very end of the hall and his long strides became a familiar comforting sound. Then my day nurse would show up to take my vitals. I would wait impatiently for Lee to visit. He would bring with him a cup of coffee and a buttered hard roll. Sometimes he would play on the computer and other times he would take a nap. I watched a lot of TV. I tried to read, but my concentration was in the shitter. Ha, figuratively and literally. I would have some visitors in and out and I would doze off now and then. The routine made the hospital a little more like home and I became more comfortable with my surroundings every day.

I refused to ever let anyone close the curtains in my room. That's part of the reason I think I woke up so early. I loved seeing all the beautiful colors in the sky as the sun came up every day. It was the most stunning sight. I needed to see that every day. I had to see it every day. Not knowing if my last days were right around the corner, made me have to see the beginning of every new day. It wasn't some grand poetic gesture, it was how I felt. Sleep wasn't my concern, survival was my concern. There was a middle school outside my window and I enjoyed watching the parents drop their kids off and pick them up from school. I was envious of that simple chore. I would have given just about anything to be able to drive my son to school. I would think about how lucky they were and I wondered if I would ever be able to do that again. I cried watching them. I missed my son terribly. It was the simple things I missed most of all. Like hearing all about Bill's day on the car ride home and if he had a bad day making him tell me one good thing that happened that day to change his mood. Who was there for him now? I felt guilty for getting sick.

Chapter 12
Hospital Experiences

I did have a few really bad days in the hospital. The chemo gave me extremely bad heartburn almost to the point where I thought that I was having a massive heart attack. Nothing the nurses gave me helped. I couldn't lie down and the pain went on for hours. Finally I was given some kind of liquid medicine that tasted like yuck and the pain began to subside that was until the nausea set in. I was on the phone with a friend and I had to rush off because I knew the throwing up was about to begin. I kind of didn't care though, because I only wanted this feeling to go away. I was looking for a puke bucket and I realized I didn't have one so I grabbed my garbage can and ralphed in it for what seemed like forever. Wow that was awesome, I felt one hundred percent better! I buzzed for my nurse and said I was throwing up. She came right into my room and she was so annoyed that I threw up in a garbage can. You see, I wasn't allowed to touch anything that had touched the floor. If I dropped something, it had to stay where it was until it could be wiped off and I friggin puked in a garbage can. Germs galore!!! Anyway, after that they always made sure I had a little throw up container near me, but that was the one and only time I threw up during induction. Oh and that horrible pain went away once I threw up.

Then came the morning that changed my life forever. I woke up to my usual routine. I did the potty and computer thing and I was lying in my bed watching a morning news show. I was all cuddled up in my hospital gown and my cotton red with white polka dot jammie pants. My cat comforter from home was on my bed and pictures that my friends' kids had drawn for me were taped over the stupid hospital flower pictures. Right on time I heard the familiar footsteps of Dr Friend heading toward my room. Hmmm, everything sounded a little more urgent this morning. Dr Friend and I said our usual salutations of "hi friend," "hi friend." I picked up the phrase "hi friend" from my sister Melanie. She had been saying that to one of her friends for years and for some reason I felt like it fit my situation. I really did and do feel like my oncologist is my friend. So, Dr Friend proceeded to sit on my bed near my legs and touched my left calf as if there was some big news. My head was about to explode. Holy shit, isn't the chemo working? It's amazing how quickly a dozen horrible thoughts can enter your brain and cause panic. Dr Friend said, "One of your sisters is a perfect bone marrow match!" I was shocked and I asked, "which sister?" He said, "Melanie." My initial reaction was to crack a joke and I said, "Thank god I'm not going to be a lesbian! Oh no, I'm still going to be a Democrat." We both chuckled until the magnitude of what Dr Friend had just said to me set in.

I burst into tears. I think it was the first time any doctor had seen me cry. This wasn't a gentle sob. This was a full on heart wrenching, body trembling, shoulders heaving, can't catch my breath, not able to say a coherent word melt down. I couldn't believe the words I just heard! Could something good be happening? I was so used to only hearing bad news that my body and mind finally released all the negativity into a hurricane of tears. I stopped being strong for a little while. The odds hadn't been on my side. When I called Melanie to tell her the news I was still crying uncontrollably and I have no idea how she understood one single word coming out of my mouth. But she did and she told her husband Jack what all the commotion was about and she started crying too. My sister, Marlene, actually felt sad that she wasn't my match and she quickly joined in our sob-fest. It had just been the three of us in one way or another forever and this was no exception. I needed both of my sisters at this time and they didn't disappoint. I think everyone in my family felt in his or her hearts that my life had been saved. For the next couple days, the nurses were coming to see me and say they heard the good news and friends were calling to congratulate me. Unfortunately, I also heard the rumblings how some people in the city were saying I wouldn't survive. So screw them! I did survive!!!

Most of my time in the hospital was pretty boring. Occasionally, I would have fun and occasionally I would be sick. I'm trying to decide which story to start with. Hmmm. I could share with you the time Mel and Marlene were visiting and Mel and I put on thong underwear over our clothes while my nurse Melissa was out of the room and she walked into the disturbing sight. No, I don't wear thong underwear! Who the hell in their right mind would want that little piece of material up their ass while they are shitting their brains out? They were obviously meant to be a gag gift. One pair was pink with red lace and the other pair was red with green lace. If unders are not cotton I don't wear them. Umm, that might be too much information. Anyway, Melissa laughed at us and she was great at understanding our sense of humor. Some nurses were more serious than others, but it was okay, I liked having the mix and I made it almost my job to make the more serious caretakers laugh. I broke most of them. Life is too short not to laugh and my life had the potential of being shorter than most, so laughter was key.

My worse night in the hospital was the night my blood pressure did a nosedive. The diarrhea was horrendous and I was too weak to get out of bed on my own. I asked the nurses aide that peeked her head in to check on me, to help me to the bathroom and I don't know if she didn't understand me or she chose to ignore me, but she just left. I had two choices, poop in the bed or attempt getting to the bathroom by myself. I got out of bed, unplugged the IV and slowly walked toward the bathroom "prairie dogging" the whole time. I made it to the toilet. I sat down and I could feel myself passing out. As my vision was tunneling, and there was no doubt that I was going down for the count. I grabbed the cord next to the toilet paper to call for a nurse. That was the last thing I remembered until I came to, still sitting on the toilet, and leaning on my nurse. She told me to stop farting and that I was farting while I was passed out. That made me laugh. You would think I would have been embarrassed, but it amused me. She knew that I would appreciate the humor while they (my nurse and another aide) cleaned me up and got me back to bed. They called in the on call oncologist that night, because my blood pressure was dangerously low. I guess that can happen with chemo sometimes and they also wanted to call Lee. I wouldn't let them call Lee because he worked about an hour away and I didn't want him to be scared and have to drive that distance. I told them that if I wasn't better when he got home from work about ten or eleven, they could call him. We never had to call Lee because I was better by the time he got home. When I was brought back to bed, I wasn't myself. A cozy, calm came over me and I wanted to sleep. Not a sleepy sleep, but a relinquishing sleep. That is the only time I have ever felt anything like that and I believe that was the closest to dying that I was through this entire process. After that incident a commode was put next to bed. Awesome sight and smells for visitors!

So, my sisters-in-law Carol and Judy came to visit one day. They both lived about and hour away. Carol was a huge gift giver and was generous to a fault. Hardly a day went by that I didn't receive a card or a gift from Carol. My very favorite gift was an angel. The angel is about fifteen inches tall, with a green and gold dress, a green sash, brown hair, gold shimmering wings and praying hands. She is beautiful. Up until this point, I was never much of an angel fan. I would joke with Mel and tell her that I wanted to rip their little wings off. I know, I know I have a very sick sense of humor and I don't feel that way anymore. I loved and still do love that angel. She would shimmer in the early morning light on the windowsill in my hospital room and I felt comforted.

Chapter 13
Break time

This is the point where I took a short siesta from my story. Bringing back all the memories has also brought back all the feelings I had at the time. I never expected this process to be so long and difficult. I'm shocked that there are days and subjects that can take me two hours to write two paragraphs. I thought that this is my story and it should be easy to write because I lived it and come to find out, it's just the opposite. In order to be true to the story, I need to be honest with how I felt and not just write how I feel about it today. They really are two different things. Reliving the horror is good and bad. I'm getting it all out and I'm learning how to take the time to remove myself from it when it's getting to be too much. And there are times when I feel like it's getting to be too much. I feel like I'm right back there being sick and it takes some time for me to get back to the present day. Sometimes writing this book scares me and I start to worry about the "c" word coming back. I assume and hope that is all the nature of the beast.

I also had to take a break because I lost a friend to MDS two weeks ago. I'm involved with two different organizations that connect survivors with someone beginning their voyage through the maze of treatment. Cathy was a woman that I had been talking to for a couple of months and we really formed a bond. We had made plans that she was going to come to Connecticut after she recovered because she wanted fresh seafood. Cathy lived in the Midwest and only was able to get frozen seafood, so I was planning a trip to Mystic, CT for next summer. Her brother was a perfect bone marrow match and I believed with all of my heart that she was going to be fine. She had a wonderful attitude, a great sense of humor and she was full of life. Initially Cathy was doing well, but then there were infections and a stroke and my friend's life was cut short. Although I never met Cathy in person, I feel like I had known her forever. Her daughter called me on a Saturday afternoon to tell me of Cathy's passing and she sobbed while speaking to me. I tried to be strong, but I didn't know what to say to her daughter. "I'm sorry" just wasn't enough. Honestly, I was more than sorry, I was devastated. I attended an event called Light the Night that is run by the Leukemia and Lymphoma Society, just a week after I received the news about Cathy. Different colored lighted balloons are carried at night and a lovely walk takes place. It's a beautiful sight. Red balloons are for supporters, white balloons are survivors and gold balloons are in memory of a person who has passed. I carried a white balloon for myself and I carried a gold balloon for Cathy. It was difficult. I needed to wrap my head around her death. I'm still pissed about it and I still shed tears over my friend. Survivor's guilt is a real thing, but that's for another time.

There are often things about the first hospital that haunt me to this day. The scent of certain antibacterial gels can bring me right back to the hospital. I've actually had a physical reaction to the smell. I have been an absolute mess and done everything in my power not to burst into tears, just because of a gel. I also had a favorite perfume, but one of my nurse's aides wore the perfume (by the buckets) and now I can't stand to be around anyone who is wearing the scent. I even gave away an expensive bottle of it, because I'll NEVER wear it again. I don't think that anyone working around patients should be allowed to wear any cologne or perfume or any smelly stuff. It can really mess with your head. That's beside the fact that many patients in the hospital feel like barfing quite often and that smell only makes it worse. It really should be a strictly enforced policy for the comfort of the patients, but that's just my opinion.

Chapter 14
Some of My Visitors

There were quite a few unusual things that happened during my induction therapy at the local hospital. First of all, a friend of mine thought it would be a good idea to ask a Reverend friend of hers to visit me. Normally, I would appreciate the gesture, but this guy was a nut. The chemo had begun to kick in and was causing uncomfortable intestinal issues, so having a stranger in my room wasn't something I especially cared for. Initially, this guy wanted to pray with me and I figured that a couple prayers wouldn't hurt, even though I wasn't on speaking terms with God at the time. I kept thinking to myself, if I pray with him maybe he will go away soon. NOPE. We prayed and then that guy proceeded to talk about himself for two friggin hours. I wanted to rip the IV out of my arm and stab him with it!! He wasn't there for me, noooo, he only wanted to tell me how wonderful he was. I couldn't wait for him to leave and I called my friend and told her that I NEVER wanted that man in my room again. I'm sure he had no intention of coming back, because he already had told me about his entire life, so he was on to his next victim. I ran into him a few months later and he had no idea who I was. Hahaha! Of course he didn't know me, he was too self absorbed.

After my encounter with Mr. Wonderful, Lee and I decided that there would be no more random visitors. A note was taped to my door saying that although I appreciated everyone's care and concern, I needed my rest and I needed to keep germs to a minimum. Lee, my sister Mel, and Kar were the only people who could waltz in whenever they wanted. Anyone else had to check at the nurses' station or they needed to call ahead of time. Believe it or not this did ward off at least one visitor that I barely even knew from entering my space. So one day, soon after we placed the note on my door, a nurse came in to tell me that two members of the City Council were there to visit. I was feeling pretty good that day so I said okay. In walk my two friends, one of which was wearing a fake nose and mustache, just to make me laugh. I did laugh and we had a very nice visit. I think I still have the fake nose and mustache somewhere. I told them both that I would see them at the February Council meeting and they gave me that, yeah right, kind of look. I knew that they thought there was no way in hell that they would actually see me there. I wasn't so sure either, but that was my goal. I needed to set goals along the way and that was one of them.

One day I received a phone call from my nephew, Michael. He is my sister Marlene's oldest son and he asked if he could come for a visit. Michael and I are only eight years apart in age, so it's not really an aunt, nephew relationship. Michael lives in Maryland and he's an attorney. He had some legal business to take care of on the border of Connecticut and Massachusetts so he rented a car just to come and see me. Can you imagine? I loved our visit, because he shared with me all about his wife and kids and what everyone was up to. Those are the kind of conversations that kept me going. His brothers Mark and Jimmy would call me and do the same thing. All three of them make me laugh and on occasion they would call me Aunt F'er, as a joke. It's a <u>South Park</u> reference.

My days were either extremely boring or filled with too much excitement. Very rarely was there ever an in-between. How do I explain this?? Well, I kept the temperature in my hospital room on the chilly side. Okay, most people thought it was really cold. My thermostat didn't work properly so my choices were yucky hot or cold. I chose cold. Someone did send a repairman to my room to fix the thermostat, but he didn't fix it and I was fine with the temperature. My visitors, not so much. I thought that the cold would kill any germs and that the heat would breed bad stuff. I needed to keep all that shit away from me. Well, the coolness in the air also caused a dry environment and the inside of my nose was icky. Needless to say, after a brief dig with my pointer finger, my nose began to bleed. Remember, I had very few platelets if any at the time so bleeding was a very bad thing. My nose bled for hours and hours.

Mel was visiting that day and couldn't believe that the bleeding just wouldn't stop. I remember being aggravated with my nurse because I felt like she was ignoring me while I was bleeding to death. I wasn't bleeding to death. I just thought I was. Eventually, the bleeding stopped, but that isn't the only bleeding story.

So, maybe a week into my hospital visit, I got my period. Men can skip this paragraph. This was definitely another one of those; you've got to be kidding me moments. Chemo, diarrhea, hair falling out and now this nonsense?! Again, no platelets so my bathroom had become a crime scene of epic proportions. This was not the every day normal period. This was nonstop bleeding with clots that looked like plums. I was exhausted. They called in a gynecologist to make sure that there weren't any additional issues, and all was fine, just annoying. All this loveliness was captured in the thing in my toilet that they called a hat. Hmmm, is that where the old expression, shit in your hat came from? Maybe that was just something my grandmother said and not a well known expression. Nothing is sacred when you are in the hospital and I mean nothing. Everything is measured, weighed and kept track of, even when you crap in your bed. Those poor nurses and aides!

There was a young woman who came into my room every morning to clean. She would mop the floors and dust and clean the crime scene area. When my hair began to fall out she would tape a small white bag to the side of my bed so I could put all the hair from my pillow into it. She would smile at me and say, "Here miss," and I would thank her every day. That might appear to be a small gesture, but it was huge to me. I believe she was trying to make the experience of losing my hair as easy as possible. I kept tape by my bed to get up all of the hair. Sometimes it would get itchy or go in my mouth when I slept so I tried to keep my pillowcase clean. I didn't mind losing my hair as much as most people. It was just another part of this never-ending "c" word voyage. I began to wear a light blue, almost gray hat, when the hair loss became noticeable. The American Cancer Society gave me a free wig. Two elderly ladies came into my room with a few wigs for me to try on. They were kind and also "c" word survivors, but not wig experts. I kept a couple wigs in my room and tried them on for Lee, Mel and Kar and eventually, I settled on a human hair wig. Those things are uncomfortable, but they do their job. At least I could wear it when I needed to be out in public and it really was a very good quality wig. They also gave me a couple wig catalogues in case I wanted a different style or whatever. I know this part is difficult for many people and I really can't explain why it wasn't as bad for me as it is for many women. Maybe I accepted the demise of my hair early on in my diagnosis, or maybe I was too afraid of everything else to also add another fear onto my plate.

Chapter 15
Faith

There was one night when I was feeling kind of down. I didn't feel like my numbers were going up fast enough and I was sick of transfusions. They gave me hives and then I had to be pre-medicated which made me drowsy and grumpy. I didn't even want to do my little ritual. My ritual was as follows; at least three times a day or more I would ask for protection, take a deep breath while picturing a white light entering my body and then I would exhale dark gray blocks. I would take a second deep breath while picturing a white light in the blood throughout my body and then exhale gray blocks. During my final deep breath the white light would surround my body to keep all bad things away and I would picture the gray blocks going away in more of a dust. I have no idea where I came up with this visualization, all I know is that it worked for me. It calmed me down and allowed me to let a healing light into my body and life. The reason I did three breaths was for the Holy Trinity. My Catholic beliefs and upbringing sneaked in even though I was not on good terms with God directly. I guess I wasn't mad at all religion and faith, but I did have many questions. Like the inevitable, why me?

I didn't feel like watching TV and I was kind of just sitting there waiting for the night shift nurses to come in to take my vitals and fix my IV. I swear that damn thing had a mind of its own. I think it kinked itself just to torture me. Suddenly, I saw these pulsating shapes on the wall behind my IV pole. I checked to see what could be causing these images and I couldn't find a thing. No glasses of water, I was in a tower so no street lights, not the TV, I was baffled. They were different shape lights, some square and some round. Their colors were muted gold, brownish, and greenish with almost a halo effect around them like the moon on a hazy night. There were maybe six of them, I think. They looked almost like a water reflection in their movement and all of them together took up about eighteen inches in diameter. They stayed for a while and I believe with all my heart that they were my angels. I said the words "thank you" out loud as a few tears of gratitude trickled down my cheeks. I knew they were watching out for me, whoever they were.

Later that night, I told my nurse's aide (actually she was just like my nurse) what had happened. She told me that other patients have told her that they had see things like that too. The next day Mel came to visit. My sister doesn't believe in "any of that shit" as she would say, so I didn't bother to tell her of my other worldly experience the night before. We were sitting there talking and laughing and I'm sure we were making fun of something, when she got a weird look on her face. Mel kept glancing past my head to the wall behind my IV pole. She would slightly tilt her head to one side to get a better look. Then her eyes were checking for the source, but she didn't say a word, she just kept looking. Finally I said to her, "So, do you see it too?" She said, "What the hell is it?" I told her to just say hi. Reluctantly she said hi. I suppose we both needed to see the angels, because they never appeared again. I felt oddly comforted by my visitors, whoever they were.

Some people may think that all of that is a big load of malarkey, but I know what I saw and what I felt. Something or someone was watching over me. Looking back, things like that happened to me at many junctures. I was being guided and taken care of by some unknown source/sources. People who could help me were put in my path every step of the way, just like the person who told Lee that I needed a second opinion. Or Dr Friend having just met my Boston doctor, a specialist in MDS two weeks before my diagnosis. Or Mel being a perfect bone marrow match. Or the many other coincidences that happened without explanation.

Chapter 16
Stuff

I took advantage of anything the hospital had to offer to their "c" word patients. There was a nurse who did reflexology. She concentrated on my feet and legs. I need to explain that I have a serious aversion to feet. I hate seeing most people's feet and I hate anyone touching my feet. Pedicures are not for me! I don't think that any man should ever and I mean ever wear flip-flops, other than beach wear. Women who wear open toed shoes had better have some decent looking feet and toe nail polish. No crooked toes or Frito toenails. I understand that some people don't care what their feet look like and they are more into comfort, but nasty looking feet make me gag a little. So as you can tell, the thought of someone touching my feet was a huge stretch for me. I painted my toenails red before I went into the hospital, knowing darn well that people would be looking at my feet and I wasn't allowed to cut my nails. Ugh! No sharp objects near someone who doesn't have platelets. I have no idea why I agreed to let someone fondle my feet, but I did. Needless to say, it felt wonderful! It actually helped me relax a little and it was nice for just a short time not to be poked and prodded. My body had been feeling so many painful and uncomfortable things, that just being touched gently was a welcome change. Who knew?

I had quite a cast of characters as my support system during all the nonsense. There was a woman named Pauline who was on the Council with me and she came to visit me quite often. She is a more mature woman and her personality is not like anyone else. Pauline doesn't have a filter. That doesn't just mean with the things she says it also applies with the way she cares for people. Pauline took my family under her wings during my illness and she became a mother figure for me. At 45 years old I still needed a mom when I was sick and because my own mother had passed away years before, Pauline became my surrogate mother. She brought me lemon candies to suck on because it helped her late husband with the effects of chemo and she sometimes said inappropriate things to people and that always made me laugh. I remember one time she said to a nurse, while pointing at me, "Do you know who this is? She is a very important person in this city!" I cracked up. Sometimes I would say, "Pauuuliine, you can't say stuff like that," and she would tell me that she can say whatever she wants and she did say whatever she wanted. She took good care of me and was quite the character in the process. My sister Mel said to me once that our parents wouldn't have been able to handle seeing what I was going through. I believe she was correct, so I was extremely lucky to have Pauline. She still makes me laugh and shake my head.

Another person who was instrumental through this process was my close friend Kar. She called me every day at least once and came to visit probably 5 or 6 days a week. Kar and Mel were my "go to" people. I suspect that they spoke to each other almost every day to share the latest information about my health. One freezing cold night Kar came to visit and we started playing some card game that someone had brought to me and we ended up laughing hysterically for a couple hours. There was another night that Kar came running into my room because I hadn't answered the phone and she thought something was wrong. I felt so bad seeing her so frightened and I think I was just in the bathroom for a change. She also made sure that I always had a clean comforter on my bed. Her mother gave me a floral comforter with a scalloped edge on it so the two comforters could be swapped out and I would always have something cozy on my bed. I know that my illness was hard on Kar and she was a very good friend through the whole thing. I don't know what I would have done without her. We are no longer in contact with each other, but I will forever love her for everything she did for me during this terrible time in my life. My heart holds a special place for Kar and no time or distance can change that.

Chapter 17
Doing Better

The day finally arrived when my nurse with the curly shoulder length blonde hair came into my room and said that my white blood cells went up a little. Just a little, but hurray they were starting to go up. I was getting very antsy and every day I would ask her about my numbers and every day she would say they would come up pretty soon and they did! This was a great sign. Things were starting to recover, but they needed to do another bone marrow biopsy to see if I was actually in remission. I honestly just kind of assumed that after all that chemo I would be in remission. Then I began to realize that some people don't reach remission the first time. Holy shit, I can't go through all of that again! Once was more than enough for me!!!! I wanted to get it over with. The day came for bone marrow biopsy number two. I wasn't afraid this time, because I knew what to expect. My blonde nurse pre-medicated me and I waited for the doctor to come to my room for my test. I waited and waited and no one showed up for my biopsy. I was pissed because my pre-meds wore off so I had to get them again. I hated the feeling of being slightly out of it. My nurse wasn't thrilled either. She was an amazing advocate for her patients and made sure that this time they were going to come to do the biopsy.

The first person, who came into my room, was there to prepare me for the biopsy. She had me lie on my stomach and prepared my hip for the invasion of needles. Hey, I guess this could be a form of the body snatchers. Then, many more people came into my room including the doctor who did my initial biopsy all those weeks ago. It was comforting for me to have the same doctor. I was a little loopy, for lack of a better word and I proceeded to tell everyone in the room to come around to the top of my bed so I could meet the people who were looking at my ass. Yes, I actually made them all introduce themselves and I saw all of their faces. Then they could proceed. Someone got some blood on my cat comforter and the stain is still there today and no I didn't put the comforter in the attic. I don't recall any pain that time, but I was medicated twice and I think fear is more painful than actual pain. Not the next morning, but the one after that Dr. Friend sat on my bed and told me that I was in remission!! I have no memory of telling people or making phone calls even though I'm sure that I did. I think the relief was too overwhelming to be able to retain anything else.

My appetite was slim to none. Ha, no pun intended. At one point Dr Friend decided to put me on a drug to stimulate my appetite. Okay, it's the pot pill and we were hoping I would get the munchies. There is a school of thought that all this drug does is assist in getting your appetite back without a "high" sensation.

Well I'm here to tell you first hand that I was friggin high. My son tells the story that one night while we were on the phone together I asked him why he called me. He proceeded to tell me that I called him and we both laughed for quite a while. He knew about the drugs I was on and thought it was funny that his mom was a little toasted. After a couple days of not feeling completely in control, I asked Dr Friend if I could please get off of the medication. I said, "It's not making me hungry, it's just making me high." I'm fairly positive that I said other bizarre things to people, but they were all too polite to tell me. Everyone always feels apprehensive around the poor "c" word patient. All I know is that there are a couple days in the first hospital that are hazy. Not chemo hazy or painkiller hazy, but foggy, woo hoo hazy.

I finally got the okay to walk the halls in the hospital, once my white blood cells were high enough. I was able to see the half dead flowers sitting in the windowsill outside my room that people had sent to me. I wasn't allowed flowers or fruit in my room because of bugs and germs so there were things that my wonderful friends sent to me that I never got to enjoy. Lee brought some things home, but forgot to save the cards. So thank you to the people I never said thank you to because I didn't know you sent anything. I was uncomfortable leaving my room for the first time. There were still some holiday decorations up in the hallway and I looked into the rooms to see the other "c" word patients. Some didn't look so good and some waved. I was just grateful to be out of my room. I did wonder about the other people on the oncology floor and how they were doing. Sometimes I would wonder if anyone had died that day on my floor. I'm sure people did. I couldn't allow my mind to go there very often. This one evening, I didn't have an IV connected so the nurse let me go up the hall to take a shower. I couldn't wait to wash what was left of my hair and really get clean. She got me all settled and left me alone in this giant shower. I hated it! I wasn't sure I was strong enough to do it alone and I wasn't sure that I had enough energy to get back to my room. She told me I would be fine and she was right. I needed the push to stop being so dependent on all of the staff. I was like a baby bird being pushed out of the nest. Thank goodness for incredible nurses! I gained my independence quickly after that and I was strong enough to go home. My white blood cells had reached an acceptable level, so I was able to pack up my crap and get the hell out of there.

Chapter 18
Leaving the Nest

On January 22, 2007, I was released from hospital number one, just in time for my wedding anniversary on the 28th. I had packed the biggest bag you can imagine, thinking that I would need a ton of stuff for a month long hospital visit, but in reality, I didn't need much. Lee picked me up and we headed home. It was exciting to see my dog and three cats. I had missed them and occasionally, I would ask Lee or Billy to hold the phone up so I could talk to them. My pets, aka family members, acted a little stand offish in the beginning. I think I brought home many unusual smells with me so they didn't know what to make of me initially. Soon enough they were rubbing up against me, sitting on my lap and annoying me. The biggest surprise was that all the Christmas decorations were still up including the tree. I know I told you about the food, but the decorations are all encompassing. The inside of the house was decorated top to bottom. Kitchen curtains, dishtowels, cookie jar, timer, placemats, toothpick holder and that's just the kitchen. All the bedding was switched to Christmas and the shower curtain and towels and bathmat and toilet paper. You name it, if I could find it in a Christmas motif; it was changed for the season. As I looked around on my first day home, I really wished that I hadn't decorated so much. How the heck am I going to find the energy to put all this stuff away?! I had completely forgotten that the house was decorated. I knew that Lee had absolutely no idea where to begin in the de-Christmasing of our home. UGH!! I had always loved Christmas time, but I wasn't so sure how I felt about it anymore. Now I had all these horrendous memories associated with the holidays. I wasn't sure how I would feel next year or even if there would be a next year for me. I still had to have a transplant. Crap!

My strength came back quickly once I returned home and I was actually feeling great. For the first time in quite a while, I was leukemia free. I was thinner and I had a ton of energy. Okay, I was also balder, but that's what hats were for. Lee bought me a diamond journey necklace for our anniversary that year oh, and a star necklace with small diamonds. I guess I earned it. I did get all the decorations put away with help from Lee and I cleaned everything in sight. I tried to get very organized. I figured that if I made it through the transplant process, I would need things neat and if I didn't, I wanted things to be as easy as possible for Lee and Billy. I didn't want them to have to deal with my overabundance of stuff. I went through all my cooking magazines and clothes and all the other nonsense we all tend to accumulate. Lee asked me once why I was cleaning so much and I told him to make it easier for the people who have to come in to clean before I'm allowed home from the transplant, but that was only partially true. I wasn't sure that I would return home after the bone marrow transplant. I knew that there was a chance that I might die. I was still scared and there were many times during my expunging that I would cry. I would find pictures of Billy when he was small; cards from people I love and every item seemed to hold a wonderful memory. All memories up until getting sick, seemed incredible, even the icky memories. Things that seemed earth shattering at the time were so inconsequential now. My perceptions were all different. Realistically, my perception then was probably the correct way to look at life and I remind myself of that occasionally. It's easy to slip back into the negative.

Chapter 19
Another Doctor

My first trip to Boston to a hospital a.k.a. "Man's Greatest Hospital," happened soon after my release from my local hospital. Dr Friend had been to some kind of medical thing the week before I first entered his office and at this medical thing the doctor who spoke was one of the foremost authorities on MDS. Dr Friend was so impressed by this other doctor that when he received my case he called the Boston doctor immediately to fill him in on my case. Leukemia isn't that rare, but MDS is on the list of rare disorders so it was lucky that Dr Friend had just met Dr EA. What the hell are chances of that happening? From the beginning they worked as a team for me. Dr EA was a young, handsome physician with his heart in research. Wait, did I say he was handsome? The moment I met him, I knew he was the doctor for me. Not because he was handsome, but because I trusted him. I was beside myself with nerves going to see yet another new doctor in a strange place. I was so sick of the whole thing. It seemed never-ending. All I could think was that I really hoped this city hospital wasn't like the other one I had visited. This time I would walk out! I wasn't on crutches and I wasn't sick so there was nothing keeping me from bolting if need be. I kept telling Lee that I would leave if it was dirty. End of story! Lee and I had already had a huge fight over which hospital I should have the transplant. He wanted me closer to home, but I wanted the best. I didn't give a shit if I was alone; I wanted to be where I felt like I had the best chance of survival. I knew it would be harder on all of us, but I followed the little voice inside of me, and we went to meet Dr EA.

The hospital in Boston was clean! Yippee! We walked through the halls of the new hospital looking for what they call clinic. Upon entering the clinic, there was a long reception desk on my left and lots of chairs for waiting on the right. Seeing many chairs in a waiting room are never a good sign, in my experience, but this time was different. The receptionist's name was Faith. Her name gave me a good feeling right off the bat. She was warm and welcoming and made me feel like I had known her forever, phew. I asked to use the restroom because we had just been in a car for about two and a half hours and by the time I was done going pee pee the nurse was asking for me. The nurse weighed me, took my blood pressure and temperature and led me into the room to meet my newest doctor. Lee was there with me when Dr EA came in to talk to us. He shook our hands and proceeded to show us a chart that showed survival between consolidation therapy and bone marrow transplant. Consolidation therapy is the chemo you receive after induction to support remission. I said to Dr EA that I didn't think I had a choice because of the MDS and he left the room to review my chart again. Somehow that MDS diagnosis kept getting hidden. The doctor came back into the room and said that I was absolutely right and a bone marrow transplant was my best option especially with having a sibling who was a perfect match. He also wanted to do a bone marrow biopsy while I was there to double check remission. In Boston the doctors do their own biopsies and I think they had warned me about the biopsy ahead of time.

I was wearing a black velour sweat suit because I knew it would be easier than jeans for the biopsy. I think they gave me some pre meds, but I'm not positive. I wasn't as afraid this time because I knew exactly what to expect. I also had my colorful Virgin Mary medal in a little plastic bag in my hand. The medal always calmed me down. On the other hand, Dr EA didn't expect my bones to be so hard and my muscles to be so strong and my pelvis to be tilted. He said I was like an athlete with my strong muscles and bone, not the tilted pelvis. Dr EA really worked hard for the biopsy samples that day. I'm pretty sure he was completely worn out for the rest of the day after seeing me. Most biopsies take about twenty minutes, but that one took about forty-five minutes. I was sore, but happy. Meds will do that. I teased Dr EA after that and I would always encourage him to start working out his arms before my next biopsy. I think he didn't like me being in pain. It was more discomfort than pain and I never held it against him. After Lee saw the hospital and met Dr EA he agreed that Boston was the place I needed to be for treatment. Even my stepson Matt had checked out Dr EA online and he thought it was the right place too.

Chapter 20
In Between

While I was in between hospitals, both of my sisters and my sister's partner, Donna, came to visit. We went out to dinner around the corner from my house and it was the first real meal that I had eaten since my prison, oops, I mean hospital break. Mel had baked a carrot cake with cream cheese frosting for Donna's birthday, so we had dessert back at my house. I think it was the best cake that I had ever tasted in my entire life. I think that I may have eaten most of the cake all by myself. I have to say, we laughed a lot and it was a great time. I knew that they were really worried about me, but I also knew that there was no doubt in their minds that I was going to be fine. Wait a minute; maybe they just acted that way. Either way, I definitely felt very good that night. I did kind of fear that that would be our last sister dinner, but I feared that everything I did would be my last. I smiled through everything; it was inside where all the doubt took up residence. I worried about all the people who loved me. I worried about what this nonsense was doing to them. I was glad for a good night and no worrying, if only for a short time.

Remember how I told a couple Council Members that I would be at the February meeting and they were incredulous? Well, guess what? I was at the February

City Council meeting, just like I said I would be. I remember that I was wearing brown dress pants with a brown tweed jacket. I don't recall if I was wearing a hat or a wig. The jacket had been a little snug before treatment, but it was little loose from my weight loss. That was the huge positive that came out of a month in the hospital. I walked into the caucus room and everyone stopped talking. They knew I was going to be there, because I told the people I was closest to, but I still think it was a little surprising. Boy, did it feel great to be back in my element! I have no recall as to what the issues were at that particular meeting; all I knew was that I was back for one more meeting. I had kept up on the entire goings on and all of my constituent work. I am still very proud of how hard I tried to keep up with everything through my initial treatments. It got harder down the road. I also knew that I would not be at another meeting for quite a while. As a matter of fact, I had been working on a very important ordinance and I offered to step down as the Chairperson, knowing I wouldn't be back for a while. Luckily, we were waiting to hear an opinion from the District Court and that wouldn't be happening for a bit and with any luck, I would be back by then. This was also a re-election year for local government and I had no idea how the hell I was going to pull that off. My thought process went something like this; step one, survive the transplant. Okay, there weren't any other steps. Surviving was the only step that mattered!

In preparing for the bone marrow transplant, I got it in my head that I needed a recliner for the bedroom. Everything I read said that this was going to be a very long recovery. I also figured that knowing my past bathroom issues, I needed to be close to the latrine. We only have one bathroom in my house and it is up stairs near the bedrooms. I don't want to give you the wrong idea, there are only six stairs to go up, but six stairs are one million stairs when you have chemo diarrhea. That is the truth! Lee agreed that we would look for a recliner, which somehow miraculously turned into a whole new living room set. So we took a little drive to a furniture store about an hour away. I was very particular in what I wanted. It had to be fluffy and comfortable. I was going to spending many hours with my hiney parked on this thing so it had to be just right. Just call me Goldilocks. We picked out an overstuffed green reclining sofa, loveseat and chair. The saleslady checked on delivery and she told us that it would be ten days. I looked at Lee and told him that he would have to be home because I would be in the hospital. She asked what was going on and I told the saleslady that I was going to Boston for a bone marrow transplant and she told us to wait a minute. Somehow she arranged for the furniture to be delivered in a couple days. It might seem like a small thing, but I was extremely grateful. I would be able to see the furniture in our living room. I had a need for everything to be in place when

I left. Just in case. The unknown was always lurking like a wolf hunting its prey.

I was counting on surviving, but planning for the opposite. At the time, I kept telling myself that everything I was doing was to make my home coming easier. In retrospect and in being honest, I was planning for the worst. I saw all my friends and I cooked a bunch of food. I spent a ton of time at various doctors' offices and my arms were a mess again from having my blood drawn constantly. Where's a good picc line when you need one? I was going through so many emotions every day. I would be so happy to be alive and grateful that I made it through induction therapy with flying colors. Then I would be totally pissed off that I had gotten sick in the first place and then I would be scared out of my friggin mind thinking I was going to die. Then I would think about my family and how they would handle my death. I would think how difficult it would be on my teenage son, my husband and my sisters and my whole family. Then I would think about my funeral, I even picked out a couple songs that would be sung. Then I would stop myself and tell myself that I was going to survive all of this. This mantra repeated itself in my head several times a day. I felt like I was going out of my mind. The outside world only saw the positive parts of me during that time, but I was living something quite different inside. I found myself working very hard at making everyone around me feel confident in my survival. Phrases like "I've got this" or "I'll see you soon" were common things for me to say. I sobbed inside every time I said goodbye to someone, but I smiled on the outside. It was pure torture and doubt.

Dr EA from Boston would check in occasionally and they changed my date to be admitted a couple times. I think it was because the person whose room I was supposed to inhabit was having complications or something. I didn't especially want to think of the something. Eventually I received the call that I would be admitted on February 21, 2007. Yikes! I set up the pre-admittance appointment for my sister, Mel and me. Everything was going forward and I was anxious. Yippee for anti-anxiety meds!!

Melanie and her husband Jack came to Connecticut from New York and we all drove together to Boston. Thank God for Jack having such a great sense of humor and keeping the atmosphere light in the car. Once we all found out that Mel was my bone marrow match, Jack drove her crazy about keeping herself healthy. He would tell her in his Bronx accent, "Wear a hat, your sister is counting on you." This sure was a rough entrance into our family, but Jack took his new roll very seriously. When we arrived at clinic, Lee and I were in one room, Mel was in the room next to me and Jack was in the waiting room. I could hear the nurse practitioner talking to Mel and she said something about the shots Mel had to receive for five days prior to transplant could make her sick. I started to cry when I heard that and I told Lee that I didn't want to do it if it would make my sister sick. I was ready to back out of the whole thing. I wasn't being a martyr; I just couldn't handle Mel being sick because of me. I kept saying, "Forget it, I'm not doing the transplant." I don't recall who explained to me, with a sense of urgency, that it wouldn't be bad for her, they just always tell you the worse case scenario and everything would be fine. The shots are to raise the donor's white blood cells. Jack was a nurse so he was able to give Mel the shots every day and she didn't have to go to a doctor. I still didn't like it, but what choice did I have? I was sad that I was the reason someone else was going to feel bad. I hated the whole thing and my sister better not get sick because of me!! That would have been more than I could have handled.

I finished with my appointment before Mel, so Lee, Jack and myself were hanging out in the waiting room filled with chairs, drinking coffee. Mel finished her appointment, but when she came into the waiting room she was kind of pale. There was something in her blood work that they needed to check on a little more. They asked her if she could be pregnant. My sister was in her early fifties and her husband was in his early sixties so this would have been quite the shock. Ultimately, she wasn't pregnant, but when the nurse came out and asked us if we needed anything, Jack said, "Yeah, a suicide hotline." We all laughed with tears running down our faces. Even the nurse was hysterical. When we were leaving the hospital, we passed the gift shop and all the baby things were in the windows. Of course all that meant to me was a great opportunity to tease my sister. Hey isn't that what baby sisters are supposed to do? It never entered my mind that if she had been pregnant how difficult it would be. Mel was the one who said what a terrible decision that would have been to make. You can't be a donor if you're pregnant.

So, it's been two months since my last writing session. I would like to say that the reason I didn't write was because of the holidays, but that wouldn't be the complete truth. Yes, of course it's a busy time with Thanksgiving and Christmas and I was doing quite a bit of running around and it's also the time of the year I found out I was sick. Writing everything down and reliving the memories has been way more difficult than I expected. It has brought every fear of becoming sick again to the surface. It has become not only a fear, it's also become sadness and I'm working through it. Something of this magnitude truly needs counseling. Almost eight years later and I'm still dealing with the big "c" demons and all the residual bullshit. I love the holidays so much and I struggle through the holidays just as much. There is an incredible discomfort in thinking that history may repeat itself. So many traditions associated with November and December brings wonderful memories and horrendous memories all jumbled in to one weird emotion. No one wants to hear about those bad memories, because they don't understand or they don't think you should dwell or they can't handle it. Whatever the reason is, I go through it on my own and pretend that I'm fine. Most of the time I am fine, some of the time, I'm not. I'm still scared at times!!

I've also been procrastinating because this part of my story is the transplant part. I'm trying to figure out why this is freaking me out so much and why writing this part is causing me pause. Maybe it's because I've had friends who didn't survive the transplant. This always makes me question why I've been so blessed and what am I supposed to do with this life. I don't think I was supposed to survive something like this and not do something amazing. That's a lot of pressure. Maybe surviving is the amazing thing I am supposed to do. I just don't know, I have this need to do more. That's one of the reasons for the book! I think of my friend Cathy, who passed away in September, and she inspires me. We talked about doing a book together. It's been rough so far putting all this in writing, but I'm going to keep going. As strange as it may seem, something or someone is pushing me to continue, so onward!

Chapter 20
Leaving for Boston

Here we go! The morning I left for Boston was odd. I said goodbye to Bill before he left for school and I told him that I would see him soon. I walked around the house and said goodbye to our three cats, Johnny, Marky and Meredith and our dog, Jake. Strangely enough, I had a feeling that I wouldn't see Jake again. He was an older dog and he'd been having issues with his hips and lost his hearing. I hugged him and kissed him, but I wasn't sure if my feeling had to do with the possibility of losing him or the possibility of losing my life. I studied my home, not knowing if I would ever be there again. It felt like a loss and a final goodbye. My heart was in my stomach and I was already mourning my old life. Would I ever get another chance to sit on the new overstuffed, green sofa that had just arrived? Would I ever get the chance to complain about my small kitchen again? Would my life continue and if it does, will it ever be the same? All the things that annoyed me every day, became the things I was already missing. There were so many emotions running through my head and heart!!! Some things made perfect sense and some were a little crazy. I don't remember if Lee and I had any conversations as I was preparing to leave our home and we had a long trip to the hospital in Boston to chat.

I think my mind stopped working for the two and a half hour car ride to Boston. Fear can shut everything else down. Fear robs you of yourself and your other emotions because all you can feel is fear. It sucks!! Fear also steals your memories. That can be good and bad. Good as a protection, bad when you are trying to remember things and all that is there is the memory of sheer terror.

The next thing I know happened when I got to the hospital was going to radiology to have my "triple lumen hickman" (TLH) inserted into my chest. A TLH is actually outside your skin and suchered into the chest. It almost looks like a cross with three tubes coming out of it. One tube was chemo only; the other two were for fluids, additional meds like antibiotics or nutrition for those of us who don't eat, and one to draw blood. There was something to say which line was which, but I can't seem to remember how they were distinguished. The cross part had a plastic covering to protect it from infection. Infection is a transplant patient's kryptonite!!! There was also a small tube placement mark at the bottom of my neck. It looks like I have a spot of dirt on my neck now, but none of my scars bother me at all. I have to say that all of the people caring for me were so understanding and kind that they made a very frightening situation bearable. This whole process took hours. Waiting in radiology for an IV and then operating room backups were definitely raising my stress level. Also, sitting in the waiting room in a hospital gown and robe wasn't the most comfortable. I wanted to be anywhere else, even pooping my brains out would have been better than waiting to be locked up and sick. I did get a kick out of the guy who called everyone "amigo" and every time he said it, I smiled.

The time had come to head up to the transplant floor and I knew my freedom was being taken away. The first person that I came in contact with was my nurse, Aura. Aura is on the shorter side with shoulder length dark hair and a sweet smile. She walked Lee and I to my room at the end of the hall. Right across from my room were the computers that the nurses used. Was it something about me that made both hospitals put me at the end of the hall? Hmmm? This room was not decorated as nicely as my other hospital room, but it was very controlled. The room had filtered air so the door was always closed once the process began. It looked like any other hospital room with bland walls, oxygen, IV poles, and all the other medical paraphernalia. The room used to be a double room, but now there was a chair and stationary bike where the second bed would have been. I was very grateful that the bathroom was literally two steps from my bed, especially with my previous chemo and bathroom issues. This was a huge luxury. It also had a stall shower!!! The best part was the view of the Charles River from the huge windows, even though they were all the way across the room from my bed.

Given the choice of a view close by or a bathroom close by, I would choose the bathroom. It was so close that I never had to unplug my IV, which meant I didn't forget to plug it back into the outlet. Therefore, eliminating some of beeps and annoying sounds those machines love to make.

The nurses had to go through my bag and disinfect all of the pictures and anything else that could be wiped down, including my angel statues. I had to purchase slippers that could be cleaned daily, so I bought two pairs of those plastic clogs. One pair was orange and the other pair was royal blue. I just looked at my feet and I'm still wearing the same orange pair today. I'm a little attached to them, even though they are kind of ugly. In the hospital, I was never allowed to walk around barefooted because of germs. This is another thing that I still do. I won't walk around without shoes. It's funny because I walked around barefooted all the time before the "c" word. I finished unpacking my bags and Lee left to head back to Connecticut. I think he brought the suitcase home with him. No one knew how long this stay was going to be, it could have been months. Luckily it wasn't. I'll never forget the sound of the door closing behind me. The clank of the door, and not knowing if or when I would ever leave those tired four walls. Surreal!

So, the time had come to start the "lethal" doses of chemo. Yes, they actually call it lethal! The door to my room was closed and I wasn't allowed to leave the environment indefinitely. Anyone entering my room had to leave their coats outside the room, use antibacterial gel, and put on a mask and gloves. If they even had a sniffle, they had to stay way from me. I was in lockdown. It's very difficult to explain my feelings at this time. I remember thinking that this must be how prisoners feel when they hear those heavy cell doors close behind them. I was a little empathetic to those put in prison. Not having the freedom to leave my room was strange. Not having most of my family close to me was strange. Putting my life in the hands of people I just met was strange. I was in a world of unfamiliarity. At least I knew that once I got into a routine, things would feel better. I knew this from my previous hospital stay, but I had no idea how regimented my life would become. I welcomed routine. I tried to make myself at home. I put the pictures of my family and furry family in the windowsill. I arranged my hospital tray with my cell phone, pens, pencils, a notebook, informational pamphlets and I think there was something for my lips. I learned quickly how little I really needed in this life.

Then came the overwhelming amount of information. Actually, I was overwhelmed with all the information about receiving a bone marrow transplant before I ever entered the hospital, so I chose to take it one step at a time. It was too much to absorb all at once. It was all too frightening, especially reading about all the things that can be bad about this process. All the things that could ultimately kill me. Aura explained to me that there are things that can be done to help with many of the side effects, so I felt a little better. In this hospital there was one nurse to every two patients, so the care was exceptional. The nurses told me how to shower, brush my teeth, how much water to drink, what chair to sit on, and how to survive. I listened to everything they told me to do. I had another one of those stupid hats in my toilet, but I had that baby down pat. I knew just how to maneuver myself to get the pee pee in the front part and poop in the other half. Phew, one familiar thing, even though it was something I didn't like to deal with. I settled in and tried to get myself comfortable with my new surroundings. I wasn't comfortable. I was far away from everything that gave me comfort. I just had a sore foot, how the hell did I end up where I was. Ativan (anti-anxiety med) PLEASE!!!

Like I said, chemo started quickly, but I was used to that. I know you are wondering how I was told how to shower. Shouldn't I have known how to shower? Well, not their way. First of all, I had to use surgical soap. Then I learned to wash from my head to my toes. That's not unusual, but using one washcloth for my face and throw it out of the shower, another washcloth for each arm, throwing each one out of the shower, one washcloth for each leg and so it goes.

Drying off went the same way using five or six towels. Then trying to never touch the floor with my bare feet. Sounds easy, but not so much. The nurse always stayed in my room while I showered. She would change my bed and disinfect my room, which was comforting, because I could be a little unsteady on my feet. I showered every day except one, because I had a high fever. Brushing my teeth was another one of those towel things. When the platelets drop, you have to be very careful of cuts. Needless to say, toothbrushes were too rough so I had spongy things. Again, I think it took about six or so spongy things to brush my teeth. That didn't include the two rinses for my mouth that I had to use. One of them I used three times a day and if I remember correctly, the other one I used six times a day. This was extremely important because mouth sores are very common and painful with chemo patients. I was diligent with my mouth care. I was one of the lucky ones and didn't develop those nasty sores.

There was a small refrigerator in the corner of my room near the windows. The nurses kept it stocked with bottled water and they wrote down my water intake every day. Again, water is very important because there was a bunch of really shitty stuff in my body and the water kept me hydrated and flushed some of the crap out. Other patients kept food and other drinks like Ensure in their refrigerators, but everything seemed really gross to me. I drank my water. There was one chair in my room that was designated my chair. No one was allowed to sit in it. It was cleaned daily and a clean blanket was placed on it before I could sit in it. Every Monday was chest x-ray day. My chair would be prepared and I would sit about six or more feet inside my room, facing the door, and the x-ray guy would take the picture from the hallway. It happened quickly and the door was only open for a very short time. There were lovely women who came in daily in their mask and gloves, which were changed with every room they entered, and scoured the bathroom, floors, chair rails and they made things sparkle. Some of them would chat briefly and other ones would smile and be on with their day. I always thought that that would be a difficult job, so I thanked them before they would leave my room. As I'm writing this, I'm remembering the smell of the cleaner and the surgical soap and I'm not freaking out. This is good.

My days usually began about 5:30AM. That is when the nurse would come in to weigh me, take my vitals, do a blood draw and flush the lines of the TLH. The scale was a very large floor scale, almost like the ones that veterinarians use and almost every day my weight was decreasing. At some point, after the transplant, the doctors put me on IV nutrition or TPN, because I wasn't eating at all. I hated that stuff, but more about the TPN later. There were a few mornings that I was so exhausted that I never felt the nurse take my blood pressure or draw my blood, but I still had to get my hiney out of bed to be weighed. It was the night nurse who did the early morning vitals and they knew how to be extremely quiet. I had a very hard time getting any kind of rest in the hospital, so if I was finally sleeping everyone tried to leave me alone.

I talked to Lee on the phone every morning and usually at least one of my sisters, if not both and various other friends throughout the day. One of my doctors and the nurse practitioner would come to see me to check me out and tell me what chemo was in store for me that day. Well, I was always hooked up to chemo for the first week; it was the extra boost chemos that were a little rough. Okay, they were a lot rough. The Chaplain would poke her head in and ask if I needed anything and the girl bringing around the food trays would say hi, because she knew I wasn't eating. Actually, one day the food girl put on a mask and gloves and came in to visit for a couple minutes. We had chatted early on, before my appetite disappeared and she wanted to see how I was doing. It's amazing how something like a couple minutes visit can mean so much, very sweet. I would go through my shower routine and for the rest of the day, I would doze off and watch TV.

Sometimes, I would shop online and not recall my purchases. Actually this happened a few times. My biggest purchase was a gold and aquamarine cross. I bought it because it was the birthstone of my new birthday and a cross pendant that seemed appropriate. I remember seeing the necklace and liking it very much, but I didn't think that I ordered it. That was until Lee called and asked what I had ordered from QVC. I was baffled. I told him to open the package and let me know what it was. It was the cross and it was kind of expensive! Oops! He said that I should keep it and he paid the bill. This may have happened a couple more times with small items so my warning to all patients is, don't shop while heavily medicated. Or, the time to shop is when you are heavily medicated, because no one will get mad at you and you can get some awesome shit.

My sister Marlene came to Boston to keep me company through some of the icky chemo. Mar actually took some time off from work, just so I wouldn't be alone all the time and so she would be with us on bone marrow/stem cell transplant day. In the morning, Mar would eat breakfast and then walk over to the hospital, from her son's apartment. I had purposely saved the movie <u>Chicago</u> to watch with Marlene, because I knew that it was right up her alley. She would read when I dozed off and when I was awake we would watch TV or chat about the past. Sometimes, I would encourage Mar to leave the room and go get coffee. It was very difficult to hang out in a room with mask and gloves on for any length of time. The mask is especially annoying and I could tell when she needed a break. I can only imagine how tough it was for her to be witnessing the massacre of my bone marrow, but she sat there with me anyway. I have two remarkable sisters.

My days really picked up around 5:00PM when my nephew, Jim and his wife, Justine would come to visit after work. Jim is Marlene's middle son and we are only nine years apart in age. They came Monday through Thursday without fail. Friday nights were their date night and they really needed to have that time for themselves. I know watching this whole nightmare unfold was taking a toll on both of them. I have to say that in many ways we didn't treat my room like a hospital room. We would laugh until we cried and we all acted like we always had, with reckless abandon. Jimmy and I being so close in age behaved more like friends or cousins than aunt and nephew. Very little was off limits in our conversations, and Justine is one of the quickest wits that I have ever met in my entire life. I loved hearing about their jobs and learning all of their co-workers names and just being a part of their everyday lives. It was an absolute privilege. That was one of the best parts of being sick. Jimmy even shaved his head for me and anyone living in Boston absolutely knows how cold it is there in the winter. I think Jimmy questioned his decision a couple times when the temperature dropped. It was definitely nice to go bald with someone!

Here are some examples of the craziness that ensued in my room. Jimmy and Justine would come to the hospital directly from work and usually Jim would show up first with Justine soon to follow. One night, Justine got held up a little and Jimmy was a little concerned. Remember, this was in Boston in the middle of a very cold winter and they walked everywhere. Anyway, Jimmy called Justine's cell phone and sang, in its entirety, "I Just Called to Say I Love You" at the top of his lungs. Yes, the nurses at the computers, outside my room, were serenaded by Jimmy that evening. He was also well known for pole dancing with the extra IV pole in my room. Then there was the night he fell off of my exercise bike and a doctor up the hall heard the bang and asked the nurses what the noise was and they swiftly told him that it was just Mary's room, as if things happened every day when they knew Jimmy and Justine were around. I'll admit that things did occasionally happen. Usually it was wonderful bursts of laughter. These things weren't happening simply because Jimmy and Justine were trying to cheer me up, this is how funny and entertaining they usually are. And I love them both more than words can say. These two were a HUGE part of my recovery and there is no way to truly thank them both. Love and laughter are the best medicine.

The shenanigans would sometimes continue if I were left alone for too long. I was lonely one day and I stood at the window of my door and I sang, "Nobody Knows the Trouble I've Seen" to the nurses outside of my room. I think there may have been some patients' family members around too. They were laughing and telling me to stop so they could finish their work. I guess bad singing might be a family thing. One day or maybe evening the hospital had a harpist playing in the hallway. I'm not kidding; there was honestly a harpist!! The next day a masseur came in to my room and he was working on my shoulders. He was a quiet and serious man. I think he was trying to be respectful. I decided to loosen him up and tell him about the harpist, but I added, "A friggin harpist! Can you believe they had a harpist? I was looking for St Peter at the pearly gates! What the hell are these people thinking having a harpist playing for drugged up transplant patients!!! How about a friggin fiddle and NOT a harp!!" Needless to say, the massage stopped and we were both laughing and talking about how bizarre it was. We were more relaxed, so when the massage started back up it was more enjoyable for both of us. I still can't get over the fact that there was a harp playing. I told one of the hospital people about it and she said, "Hmmm, I never looked at it that way." Really? She thought it would be soothing! It may have been soothing to people who aren't facing their own mortality, but definitely not patients on the brink. This story still makes me laugh. I've often wondered what the other patients thought about our musical visitor or if visions of angels danced in their heads.

Through this entire ordeal, Lee and I kept in touch with everyone via CarePages. This is a service that enabled us to post how I was doing and to eliminate a million emails from people wishing me well. My friends and family could sign onto CarePages, see updates and post comments. Some were funny and some were encouraging and some just said hi. It was a wonderful way to stay connected. Most of the time I was able to post myself, but there were occasions when Lee posted for me if I was having a bad day. I have been looking back at these posts to refresh my memory and keep the timeline as organized as possible, but I'm also realizing that I had more bad days then I recalled. I'm also remembering how many people truly cared and all the kind words that kept me going through the rough times. Some of those people aren't in my life any longer for various reasons, but they will always mean something special to me.

Chapter 21
Bad Chemo

I think anyone reading this either knows someone or they themselves have gone through the affects of chemo. It wreaks havoc with so many things, but there was one chemo in particular, that was unbelievably horrendous for me and I thought I was a chemo champion… until this chemo. My doctor, who I called Dr Steve even though it wasn't his name, but he reminded me of someone named Steve, came into my room the morning of February 26th and told me that they were going to give me a specific chemo on that day and the next day. The reason for the warning was that that chemo would cause the mouth and nose to burn like there were a thousand hot peppers shoved into the orifices. I was not looking forward to this newest torment. The nurse added this chemo to my IV in the mid to late morning in a steady drip and as it progressed…HOLY   SHIT!!!   The   pain   was unbearable. It truly felt like the hottest peppers in the entire world were shoved into my mouth and up my nose. I tried to eat Popsicles and just threw them up. The nurse, Lynn, who stayed with me a good portion of the time, wrapped my face in ice. You know those cartoons where an animal character has a toothache and they have a piece of cloth wrapped around their chin and tied at the top of their head? Well, that was me! I was also given a lot of morphine, but it didn't touch the pain. This went on for five to six hours and the only way to describe it was like being doused in the fires of HELL. Imagine eating the hottest chicken wing possible, multiplying the pain by one million and having it last for hours and hours. Yeah, it really sucked!! More than words can even describe. By the time the pain subsided, I was completely wiped out and I dreaded doing it all over the next day.

Dr Steve came into my room on the 27th and asked if I was ready to go through it again. I told him, if it's going to get me better, then sure I could do it again. He explained that the team wanted to try doing the drip in the IV slower this time and hopefully that would help alleviate some of the pain. I don't know how I was so good-natured at that time. Maybe I was more afraid of dying than I was of the pain. My friend Kar and her husband Dave were coming from home to visit me that day, so I told them what had happened the day before so they would be a little prepared in case the same thing occurred. It was so great to see both of them and we were having a really nice visit until Aura came in with the chemo. It started out better this time, but as time went on, the fire in my mouth and nose progressed. I suspect that this is what a bunch of ghost peppers would feel like or whatever pepper is the hottest on the scale. I may have cried from the pain or I may have been moaning or I may have been doing all of it, I don't know. I was highly medicated and my poor friends had to witness the carnage. I hated anyone seeing me like that. At one point, I looked up and saw tears running down Kar's face. Dave had tears in his eyes too and I was making my friends sad. After a while, I convinced them to leave, because they had a long ride home. The reality was, they had been through enough with me and I had to do this part alone. About an hour after Kar and Dave left, the pain began to subside and I was able to call them on their way home to tell them I was doing better. We were all relieved! The doctor was right that the slower drip helped and the really bad part only lasted a couple hours. PHEW! I was so happy that crap was over!

This was all happening in conjunction with the 24/7 chemo. I was never off of chemo except to shower for one whole week….again. Within that week I also received chemo in a lumbar puncture at the base of my spine. The doctor told me that sometimes leukemia cells like to hang out and hide in there. Lynn was my nurse that day too. All I had to do was lean over my tray and the needle was inserted into my back. It took a little while to find the spot because the Boston hospital is a teaching hospital and a new guy was learning how to do the lumbar puncture. It didn't hurt and I never minded the medical students coming into my room. They were a good diversion and they liked to talk and ask a ton of questions. They almost always had a teacher of some sort with them so I never felt like my health was compromised. Also, my nurses were on top of everything and I mean everything.

Chapter 22
Day Zero

Then came the big day. All my numbers were at zero, which hopefully meant all the MDS and leukemia were wiped out and it was time to start over. New, healthy bone marrow!! March 1, 2007 would be another birthday. Some bone marrow recipients call it their re-birthday, I call it either my bone marrow-aversary or my bone marrow's birthday or bone marrow day. No matter how any of us say it, I still expect gifts and a nice dinner. It's a day that is wonderful and difficult at the same time. I know this whole experience was a miracle and I beat many odds, but sometimes it still irritates me. Every anniversary of the illness also brings back many memories and fears.

I always celebrate my recovery and I always mourn losing who I used to be before the big "c" attacked my life. I'm not being ungrateful; I'm just being honest. I really wish none of this ever happened to me and sometimes it frustrates me. People have said that my "c" journey was a profile in courage. You know what? It wasn't!!! I had a few choices. I could either fight for my life or I could die. I could either do it gracefully and with humor or be a miserable son of a bitch. I fought and tried to do it with a good attitude because being miserable wasn't going to help anyone. The reality is, in my opinion, if it had been my time to die, I would have. It was all on the shoulders of the medical staff and the Big Guy upstairs, I was along for the ride. I've had so many friends who haven't survived this nightmare and sometimes I feel like the lone survivor. I wonder what the Big Guy's plans are for me. It better be something good! I recently commented to someone that life is different after transplant and you can't always do all the things you used to do, but it's also a time to embrace the new and different. Things I never would have tried before, like writing, have become my salvation and passion.

Anyway, back to the bone marrow day. My nurse, Lynn, came into my room that morning almost as excited as I was to have this day finally arrive. Lynn handed me what looked like a small, round, clear stone, a little bigger than a quarter with a cream colored angel inside. It was smooth on the outside and comforting to hold. She told me that she gives it to some patients on the day of transplant and I promised to give it back for the next transplant recipient. I've often wondered how many of us have held on to that angel and how many of us survived. Lynn let me keep the angel for about a week after my transplant. I'm not sure why, but she told me to hold on to it a little longer and I was happy to have another form of comfort with me at all times. This is just another example of how incredible and thoughtful all of my nurses were.

The day of the transplant is known as day zero. This is the start of the one hundred days of food restrictions and people restrictions. I'll explain that better later. My sister, Mel was in the hospital to have her bone marrow harvested and her husband Jack was with her. Our other sister, Marlene, was in my room with Lee. The transplant was supposed to take place around 1:00PM. It didn't and I was getting nervous as hell. I asked Marlene to please go check on Mel and I was having a friggin nervous breakdown. The harvesting went well and Mel went to her hotel room to rest. I think it kicked her ass and she said the worse part was not being able to move for five hours, that and peeing in a bedpan. As the afternoon continued and there were no stem cells entering my IV, I was getting more and more anxious. I'm normally a fairly even-tempered person, but not that day. I was scared and grouchy. I think I may have cried because I thought something might have been wrong with the stem cells. I knew the cells had to be brought to the lab to do whatever they do and I was thinking that they found something. If that was the case, I was a goner. I didn't just go through all this shit to have it fail. Finally, around 5:30PM, the stem cells arrived and a sense of relief came over me.

I had to be pre-medicated with Benadryl and maybe other stuff so things are kind of foggy from this point on. I remember that Lee, Mel, Jack, Marlene, Jimmy and Justine were in the room along with a few doctors and nurses. In Boston, I didn't have just one doctor. They were a team, so every transplant doctor and nurse knew my case. Also, the doctors are on the transplant floor for a month at a time. While I was getting the chemo, I had Dr Steve and after transplant I had Dr Mac and the only time I saw my original doctor was on transplant day. They all knew about all the patients. It was quite amazing. My family members were all hanging out in the large open space to the left of my bed and the doctors and nurses were standing in front of my bed with one nurse right next to me monitoring the IV. The stem cells were dark red and grossed me out a little. They weren't injected into my hip or any of the horrible painful things that people have heard of in the past, the stem cells went into my IV. Nothing invasive. The worse part was being able to taste them as they entered my body. Absolutely disgusting!!! Just the thought of being able to taste someone else's blood is nauseating. The whole process was uneventful, at least the transplant part. It was uncomfortable having a whole room full of people just staring at me so I asked if they expected something or me to implode. I may have told everyone to stop looking at me. This was not the kind of attention that most people crave, it was creepy and uncomfortable.

The mood began to lighten and we were all asking the doctors questions and joking around. I asked Dr EA how the stem cells know where to go and he replied, "They just do." It took a moment for that to sink in and just how truly awesome the human body is. "Wow" was all we could say at that moment. Then someone asked if I could pick up traits of my sister because of the transplant. Dr EA explained that I will always have to assume that I have my sisters allergies and my own and there are other things that will change, like my blood type. With that, my brother-in-law, Jack said to me, "Well, are you horny yet?" The room erupted in laughter and Mel's face was as red as the stem cells. From that point on, the conversation flowed and the joking continued. I was so glad that Jack broke the tension and everyone almost forgot what was really happening in the room. A life was being saved. The entire transplant took about an hour.

When it was over I really wanted to tell everyone to get the hell out of my room. I wasn't comfortable being around that many people and their germs. I had no immune system. I appreciated all of their love and support and now it was time to heal. Let the engraftment begin! I was so afraid of everything that I had read about graft verses host disease (GVHD) and the way my body might react to the transplant. GVHD is the body fighting the new cells. It's important to have some GVHD because this way the doctors know that the new cells are working, but I didn't want bad GVHD. It can affect your gut, skin, eyes, liver and a multitude of other things. No two people are the same when it comes to GVHD, so it's a waiting game, a very frightening waiting game. This was the critical time and every day I was waiting for the next shoe to fall. Before I left my home for Boston, I kept telling people that I was going to a spa. I would get massages and Reiki. The fevers breaking would clean out my pores and I've already described the colonics or the emptying out of the lower region. My son hated when I would joke about it, so I stopped. He was right, there really wasn't anything amusing about the thought that he could lose his mother. I was praying that the GVHD wouldn't be too bad. I needed to see my kid. I talked to Bill every night, but I hadn't seen him since I left Connecticut and I wouldn't see him until March 10th. It was torture being so far away from him. I couldn't imagine how difficult this was for Bill and Lee. I hated the thought that they might be hurting because of me. It sucked!

Chapter 23
Post Transplant

Post transplant are the foggiest of all my memories. In looking back at my CarePages, I realized that I was on morphine more then I originally thought. Which explains the lapses in memory. Reading the CarePages has reminded me of some of the more painful and frightening times. One example was the terrible backaches. My back hurt so badly that sleep was only a distant memory. The doctors tried sleeping pills and painkillers with no relief in sight. They did EKG's and lung x-rays, to eliminate anything that could be immediately life threatening and causing this pain. Finally, one morning during my morning check-up, I suggested that we try a muscle relaxer. My doctor and nurse agreed that it was worth a try and sure enough....it worked! When a body is engrafting with the new cells, many strange things can happen. Bone and muscle pain are among the common complaints. I still suffer from muscle spasms in my hips and back, even after all this time. I always remind myself that it sure beats the alternative.

I also experienced many fevers post transplant. Again, it was the body saying, "Oh no, what the hell are all these new and unusual cells doing here? I'm not sure if I like them yet!" Fevers can also be the sign of infection, so the antibiotics were flowing. The fever days were definitely the days I wanted to be left alone. I felt blah and tired. I usually didn't have enough energy to talk on the phone, watch TV or even, are you ready for this, Internet shop. Yeah, I was that wiped out. I'm fairly sure that the fevers are a contributing factor to my lack of clarity. The other problem is that I was alone most days and there is no one to fill in the blanks for me. Of course, Jim and Justine were there at night, but on those bad nights, I told them to go home after work. They had witnessed enough and they had the distinct pleasure of smelling chemo shits first hand. Wow, my eyes are tearing just thinking about the aroma!

Another side effect from the transplant was hand tremors and they scared the poopy out of me. HA! I couldn't hold a pen or do anything that required that dexterity. When I realized that I had the tremors, I was afraid to tell Dr Mac. I hated the thought of going through any more stupid tests or going on a new drug that I could be allergic to. Well, I never had to tell the doctor because he checked for it the next morning when he asked me to put my hands out. I think my left hand had the tremor or at least that is the hand I can picture now. The tremors were caused by one of my medications and it was a common side effect. Yippee, no extra tests needed!! Then the joints in my fingers kept jamming up and that crap hurt like hell. It kind of felt like the joints were dislocating and cramping all at the same time. Annoying and painful, but I was also grateful that the really bad stuff, like mouth sores, that I had read were extremely painful, weren't happening to me. The stuff happening to me wasn't a walk in the park, but at the same time none of it was going to kill me and living was the ultimate goal. Also, for some strange reason, I always thought that I smelled bad. It was a weird chemo, sweaty body odor bad smell. It drove me crazy. The nurses kept telling me that I smelled fine, but I was grossed out. They probably couldn't smell my stench because they were wearing masks or maybe they were being polite. I know that I stank like a construction worker in ninety-degree weather without the benefit of a breeze.

One afternoon, my friends Shay and Monika came to visit for a short time. Shay had some kind of business thing in Boston, so they stopped by after lunch. It was so great to see them and catch up. They brought me pictures that their two kids Alisha and Aiden had made for me. Shay filled me in on what was happening in city government. I asked Monika to call me before they came up so I could have my light blue cotton hat on and they wouldn't see me bald. It wasn't so much about seeing me bald, it was more that I felt like my baldness made other people uncomfortable. Thinking about it now, maybe I was the uncomfortable one and I never wanted to admit it. There is also the possibility that it was a little of both.

Anyway, I loved seeing my friends from home, even if they did have to wear masks and gloves. What I would have given to be able to give them both great big hugs!! I know they both felt better just being able to actually see me and witness for themselves how I was doing. I knew my looks were changing, but I was still my feisty old self and that's what my friends were wondering. The "c" word wouldn't get the best of me.

Being bald wasn't terrible. It saved on shampoo! All my hair was gone except for three stands of red hair on the top of my head. It drove my sister Marlene and Lee crazy. That's why I left them as long as I did. It was my one way to be a little mischievous and annoying. I eventually did cut those three holdouts. One of my friends asked me if I was bald everywhere. The answer to that question was that I was hairless. I had some eyebrows left, but that was it. It's amazing how different skin can look without and hair on it. Every birthmark was so much more visible and my skin was very soft. No friction from the hair. The very worst hair loss were my eyelashes!! Not because of vanity, but because eyelashes keep all the dust and crap out of your eyes. It didn't bother me in the controlled environment in the hospital, but when I returned home, every speck of dust and every random flying piece of fur found their way into my eyes. That drove me crazy and it was uncomfortable. I did become a master of eyeliner and no one looking at me could tell that my eyelashes had jumped ship. I also discovered eyebrow pencil to fill in the sparse eyebrows. I had to buy all brand new makeup because of bacteria, but that was just another reason to Internet shop. Woo Hoo!!!

March 10th, the day I finally would see my son, Bill! I probably talked about him incessantly and all the nurses and staff knew that I was finally going to see my baby. The night before the visit, I gave Bill the rundown. He needed to shower in the morning before the visit and he would have to disinfect and put on a mask and gloves before entering my room. I didn't want him to be scared or shocked by what was happening, so I tried to prepare him for the rituals. That day I'll never forget, I could see Lee and Billy through the glass in my door, cleaning their hands, putting on the gloves and eventually masking up. When Bill walked through the door, all I wanted to do was hug him and kiss him and hold him forever, but I wasn't allowed to touch him. As a matter of fact I wasn't allowed to touch anyone until June. It sucked, but I could finally see him!! He looked great and he was with me if only for a little while. He didn't seem to mind the mask and gloves too much and I know how annoying they are to wear. We chatted for a while and then Bill wanted to watch a movie. Lee sat in one of the regular chairs and Billy curled up in the comfy reclining chair. It was the first time we were all three together in what felt like an eternity. The only other time I saw Lee was on transplant day. They both closed their eyes and took a little nap. I sat on my bed and glanced at them sleeping and all I could do was smile. I missed home!! I had been in Boston for almost three weeks at that point and I only wanted my white blood cells to start going up so I could go home. The beginning of 2007 was spent mostly in hospitals and this crap was getting old. I wanted to go home! I wanted to leave the hospital with my family that day. I wanted my life to be normal again. Like that was ever going to happen.

The days of doctors and nurses and being sick were really taking a toll on me at this point. Although, I did enjoy the days when the med students came into my room. Not only did it break up the monotony, it was just plain amusing. I loved seeing snippets of what doctors are as regular people before they become doctors. I kind of took joy in witnessing the insecurity, because that is not something seen very often once the MD comes after their names. There was one afternoon when a student came into my room with other students and the head teacher/physician. I had seen this student before so I was fairly comfortable. He was reviewing my case with the other eager young people and then he went to check my triple lumen hickmen sight. He pressed around where all my tubes entered my chest and he said to the group that there would be puss if an infection were present. I stopped him and looked at the teacher and said, "That's not true, I don't have white blood cells, so you check for redness. Don't you need white blood cells for puss to develop?" The teacher/doctor glanced at his students and said that I was absolutely correct. I cracked up! The teaching student wasn't amused. I felt bad for correcting him, but I thought that was important. It's amazing what you can learn lying in hospital beds for weeks at a time. I know way more hospital jargon then I ever imagined I would need to know.

There was another day when a doctor from Harvard asked if his student could interview me about my medical history for part of her final exam. She was a petite young woman with long black hair. The Harvard doctor looked exactly what you would think a Harvard physician would look like. He was a distinguished tall man with white hair and he intimidated me slightly. The student stood near my bed and the teacher sat in a chair at the foot of my bed. She asked me a million questions about family history, etc. Eventually, I got a little bored and I began to just be me. I was answering the questions bluntly and was joking around telling them the funny stories associated with my hospital stay. I told them the harp story with all of colorful words and inflections added. The student was laughing so hard, she was holding on to the end of my bed and the teacher/doctor was wiping the tears from his eyes. It took us a while to reel ourselves back in and continue the final, but we kept randomly laughing. It was one of those laughs when you just can't stop. When the time had come for my visitors to leave my room, they said goodbye, wished me well and the teacher looked at me and told me that I was going to be "just fine." I think they wanted to hug me, but that couldn't happen. Believe it or not, it was a fun afternoon.

Through all of this, I developed high blood pressure. I don't know why, I guess it's one of those things. I also had to have many blood transfusions, which I hated because I could taste the blood. Grrr! Then there were those pesky platelets. The doctors gave me a couple platelet transfusions, but they weren't holding. Platelets taste really nasty too, they looked disgusting and I always got hives from them, so more Benadryl for me. The platelets needed to hold so I wouldn't bleed to death. Dr Mac came in one morning and said they were going to call in specific people with even closer platelet matches to mine, but there were only two people on the registry that they could call for me. They needed to be called in soon and they may not even be available. CRAP! I was pissed! I didn't like any setbacks. I asked Dr Mac if I could have one more day and he said, "Okay, do whatever you do." That day and night I breathed in the white light and I practiced my form of faith many times over the next 24 hours. I pictured my platelets recovering on their own; I pictured every part of every blood cell to be healthy. The next morning when Dr Mac returned for his daily visit, he told me that for some unknown reason my platelets were slightly up. I laughed at him and said, "Ha, I told you that I could do it." He shook his head at me and he may have even thought I was a little kooky, but it got the job done. Come to think of it, many doctors would shake their heads at me. Not because I amazed them, but because they found me to be a little off the beaten track. I'm used to that reaction and being different only makes me more interesting. At least, that's my story and I'm sticking to it.

I had one of my most embarrassing moments during one of my daily visits with Dr Mac. Not to be graphic, but the doctors need to check for hemorrhoids occasionally. This one morning in particular I had my ass check with the doctor and nurse. I was lying on my side with my bare butt facing both of them, when the doctor poked at a bulge near the poop shoot. They were in very close proximity when a sound emitted from that region. It wasn't a loud fart; it was more of a pffffttt sound. Kind of muffled, but loud enough and long enough to hear. Yes, I'll admit, I farted right in their faces. I know that they are used to stuff like that, but I don't normally release gas in people's faces. I gave out a little giggle, but they pretended that nothing happened. How the heck do you pretend that someone didn't just gas out your face? Granted they were wearing masks as a barrier. I just know that one of them went home and told their family about the patient who farted directly into their faces and they all had a good laugh. Either that or it was told at their patient meeting with the team and a warning was issued about the flatulence. I mean, my family and I are still amused by the story and it has been repeated at many family gatherings. Looking back on it, I don't think anyone checked for hemorrhoids again. It may have been a bad fart with a lot of hang time.

Friday, March 16, 2007 was a snowy day. I couldn't even see the Charles River out of my window. Actually, there was very little visibility at all. Sometimes, the hospital helicopters would come past my window, but there was nothing that day, just snow falling quietly. I love snow, so this was making me very happy, except for one thing. My stepdaughter from Pennsylvania and my niece from Syracuse were both traveling to Boston to visit me on Saturday. I kept calling people to see if they had arrived at their destinations safely. I also wasn't feeling very well. It was probably one of the ickiest weekends I had while in the hospital, at least the ickiest that I'm able to recall. The next day was St Patrick's Day, so I made sure that my shamrock pin that my sister-in-law Carol had sent to me was ready on my table for the next morning. I was having lots of visitors and I wanted to be festive.

Happy St Patrick's Day! I felt like doo doo, but I had no intention of letting my family know how bad I was feeling. I even had to have some kind of ultrasound later that day, but for the life of me, I can't remember what it was for. Anyway, the first wave of visitors were Lee, Billy, my stepson, Matt and his then girlfriend now wife, MaryBeth, and my stepdaughter, Missy. I can't even put into words how wonderful it was to see them all. It was the weekend, so I didn't have my regular nurses, so the weekend nurse came in and told me there were too many people in my room. I told her that they were my kids and they weren't leaving. I explained that they had all traveled and we needed to be together. She said it was fine for a little while longer. I felt kind of bad because I don't think that anyone really knew what to say to me and I wasn't my usual jovial self. We tried to act normal, but nothing about the whole situation was normal. Because I was feeling so crappy, I told them to go get some lunch plus I needed to rest before my next visitors. We all needed some time to process. It was the first time that some of my family had seen the effects of the illnesses and it may have been jarring. Melissa gave me one of her rings so she would always be with me. It's a mystic topaz surrounded by small diamonds and set in yellow gold. I never took the ring off until I gained weight and sausage fingers appeared. It was an extremely thoughtful gift and it's one of those things that I truly treasure.

I closed my eyes for a short time and then my niece, Meredith (Mel's daughter), and her then boyfriend, now husband, Andy came to visit. Meredith told me that her brother, Johnny, sent his love and that he was always checking on my condition. Johnny was in college in upstate New York so I knew it was impossible for him to visit. I had only met Andy once before at my sister's wedding, so I wasn't sure if he would feel comfortable in this environment. He was fine. Andy started reading an article from the newspaper about a woman who threw hot water on her boyfriend's genitals and the boyfriend was in the same hospital as me. Someone made a joke about great balls of fire and the jokes continued from there. That was the moment I felt like Andy was going to fit in perfectly with our family of loons. They stayed for awhile and then they went to Jim and Justine's house to begin their St Patrick's Day drink-a-thon. I mean we were in Boston and it is their national holiday! Wow, was that an exhausting and exhilarating day! After that weekend of feeling like a big pile of poo, my numbers started to climb. I think part of it was timing and a bigger part of it was seeing so many people that I love. I needed that push.

On March 19th, our wonderful dog, Jake had to be put to sleep. Although I have shared so much of my life during my illness, I'm going to keep the details of that day to myself. It's still too difficult to relive and it was a very private time of grief for my family and myself.

My final week in the hospital entailed a ton of testing and getting me off of IV's. They weaned me off of my TPN, IV nutrition, and said that I had to prove that I could eat. The doctors knew that I disliked the TPN. It was a yellow puss color and it looked thick in the IV bag. I also didn't like the taste that it left in my mouth. So I ate five cheerios at a time and hid the rest. I would listen for the doctor to walk down the hall or I would see him gown up to see the guy next door and I knew to get my cheerios ready. I know that it was a terrible thing to do, but I wanted to get my hiney out of there and eating was disgusting. Everything tasted metallic. It had gotten to the point where I never even thought of food or hunger. This went on for months. My paperwork said that I had anorexia, if only they could see me now! I showed them up! Anorexia, my big, fat ass!!

Chapter 24
Learning to Crawl

Toward the end of the week a physical therapist came in and said that we were going to walk around the transplant floor. I needed to wear a mask and gloves during this exercise. This was the day I had been waiting for, for a long time. I would watch other patients walk around with their IV poles and I knew that they would be leaving the hospital soon. We would always wave and smile at each other. Their accomplishment was also my accomplishment. We seemed to have an unusual bond between people who had never even spoken to each other. Every time one of us was allowed to walk around outside of our rooms, meant hope for the rest of us. I was scared to death to leave my room, but I got ready and walked out the door for the first time in four weeks. It was equally exciting and terrifying. I made it around once the first time and I waved at all the patients still left in their rooms and I thought that maybe I was giving them hope just like the young woman in the pink turban and fluffy robe gave to me when she walked past my door. The worst part was getting used to breathing with the mask on. I learned it quickly because for the next one hundred days I wouldn't be allowed to go out in public without wearing a mask and gloves. I didn't have any energy. Zero, Zip,

Nada! I kept thinking that this whole thing was going to be a much longer road then I previously thought.

There were more rules to being discharged from the hospital then you could ever imagine. My home had to be cleaned top to bottom before I could be released. Luckily for us, our friends Cheryl and Sherri offered to help us out and from what I've heard they worked their butts off to have everything prepared for my homecoming. The curtains had to be sent to the dry cleaner, the refrigerator had to be cleaned out and no stone could be left unturned. Every floor, counter, the bathroom were all disinfected, along with all the furniture moved and cleaned under. This was a major undertaking and I'll never forget what our lifelong friends did for us. My house hadn't been that clean...ever! This all had to be done just a day or two before I returned home so time was of the essence. At first I didn't think Lee was taking it seriously about the cleaning and that it needed to be done before my arrival home, but he absolutely got it. The doctors said they wouldn't release me until it was spic and span. Realistically, they would have never known how clean my house was and I think they were stressing how important it was for my health.

The nurses taught me how to flush my own lines because the visiting nurse would only be coming to my house every seventy-two hours to change the dressing on the TLH. It was bizarre doing it to myself, but it quickly became second nature and just another routine to follow. The nutritionist visited me and told me about the special anti-microbial diet I needed to follow. I wasn't allowed to eat any restaurant food, any fresh vegetables, most fruits, and pepper because it comes from a plant, but none of this really mattered to me. Food was icky.

Another nurse came in and reviewed all of my medications with me. I was taken off of all my IVs about mid-week and I had begun to take my meds by mouth. A chart was filled out with the times at the top of the chart and the drugs in the left hand column. It was a lot. The nurse also wrote down what each medication was for. There was an anti-fungal to prevent infection, blood pressure med, something to prevent shingles, another pill to protect my liver, daily antibiotics and an anti-rejection medication. My anti-rejection drug had to be mixed with something else because it tasted like feet. Not that I know what feet taste like, but you get my drift. It took a while to find the right combination. Some patients liked to mix it with chocolate milk, but my gag reflex kicked in when I attempted that. Other patients drank it straight down, but I preferred mine with orange juice. The anti-rejection drug had to be refrigerated, only mixed in glass because it would stick to plastic and the dosage changed according to my blood work. Needless to say, I walked around with a lunchbox containing orange juice, medication, a glass and spoon and an icepack. Oh and all the other stuff I needed to take in the front pocket of the lunchbox. I was a walking, talking (maybe too much) pharmacy.

Chapter 25
Freedom at Last

Sunday, March 25, 2007 was the day I was released from the Boston hospital. It was a weird feeling. As much as I wanted to leave, I also wanted to stay. I was sooo afraid to be away from the safety of the hospital. It wasn't even like I could easily get back to the hospital if I needed to and I trusted all the people who had taken such wonderful care of me. I knew that I would be back in a couple days, but that would be a clinic visit. I would not be going back to the transplant floor where all my friends were. I even had the honor to meet one of my nurse's mother and sister. They gowned up and came to my room to meet me. Yeah, that's how close I felt to all of them. I trusted these people with my life and leaving them was beyond frightening. It was a fear medically and a sadness personally. I said goodbye to everyone when they had their last shift with me as their patient. I got teary every time. There are no words to thank every oncology nurse that cared for me. They are an amazing breed of people, filled with love, compassion and a ton of knowledge. For almost five weeks they were a part of my family and they will forever be a significant part of my life.

I woke up that morning, raring to go. My nurse came in early for my shower so I could be discharged by noon. I finished getting myself together and going through my shower ritual for the last time. No more six washcloths and towels for me. I did need to have Lee buy white towels for me so they could be bleached and they had to be washed separately from the family towels. I still insist on my white towels and I wash… okay Lee washes them separately. For some reason he likes to wash them and blankets. Weird. Anyway, I still had to pack and it's funny how much you can accumulate even while in the hospital. I folded all my clothes neatly and it was a small step to normalcy. I only wore hospital gowns and pants, but I still had all the other stuff with me, just in case. Jim and Justine came to give me a hand getting ready and I hated leaving them. Our bond was undeniable. By the time Lee showed up, I was ready to go. Well, not really ready, but I was leaving.

I put on my cotton hat; my mask and my gloves for the two and a half hour ride home. The nurse gave me an anti-anxiety pill to put under my tongue to help me with the trip. There was a lot of discomfort with the thought of leaving my protective bubble. I hadn't smelled fresh air in such a long time and I also knew that if I breathed in the wrong thing, I could get very sick or die. I needed to start getting used to the outside world, but it felt like such a threat to me. Hat, check. Mask, check. Gloves, check. Wheelchair, check. Time to face the world. I didn't want to face the world. It was a scary place for me. Jim and

Justine stayed with me at the front door while Lee went to get the car from the parking garage. I'm not sure if I was physically shaking at the thought of going through those doors, but I was jiggly on the inside. The moment the doors opened, I felt the air around my body and the sun on my face. I may have been scared, but feeling fresh air was unbelievably incredible. Then, reality hit and I only wanted to be in the safety of the car. Things were more controlled in there. I said goodbye to Jim and Justine with tears in my eyes and I kept saying thank you to them. They were wonderful caregivers and I loved the experience of being a part of their every day lives.

I sat in the passenger seat in the car and I was exhausted! That was more activity than I had had in forever. I spoke to my sisters on the way home and I may have spoken to some friends and I dozed off occasionally. We were close to our exit and my cell phone rang and it was the mayor calling to say welcome home. I guess Lee contacted him to tell him about my homecoming. It was nice to speak to him and catch up a little. As we pulled onto my street, everything looked different to me. It felt like I had been away for a very long time, but it was just that life went on without me. As we approached our house I was getting more and more excited. Wait a minute there was something very large on our lawn. It was one of those big wooden signs that people put up for birthdays and baby births, but this one was for me!! It was a giant bouquet of red roses and it said, "Welcome Home, Mary!" Now these were the kind of flowers I could be around. I started crying and I don't know how Lee kept his secret all the way home. It was the greatest gift EVER! For the next week or so, people would drive past our house and beep their horns to say hi. We live on one of those cut through streets so the giant sign got a lot of attention. I often wonder if the neighbors were getting pissed about all the horn honking, but they all knew the situation. I would wave my arms at the beeping cars to say hi. At least it was some kind of connection with the outside world. I was emerging from my cocoon.

That entire day was overwhelming! I walked into the house and the cats ran away from me. All those weird hospital smells! I called to Bill and he ran upstairs to say hi. It was killing me not to kiss his face like I did when he was a little boy. I missed him so much. I missed Lee so much. I couldn't believe that I was sitting in my living room with my family. I never thought this day would come. As thrilled to be home as I was, I also felt like a stranger in my own home. I couldn't do the simple things that I could do before I went to Boston. The bathroom, that was only up five steps, seemed like it was a mile away. The kitchen was only good for grabbing a bottle of water. Other than those few things, the couch was my friend. Maybe my best friend. It was great to see the new couch again. It had only arrived a few days before I left, so the living room looked new to me. I got comfy and took a nap. That night was the best sleep. It had been so long since I was able to sleep through the night and not be woken up at five-thirty to be weighed, have blood drawn and have my vitals checked. ZZZzzzz!

It was time once more to develop a routine to make me feel at home and comfortable. This time it was easier said than done. I was constantly at one doctor or another. I saw Dr EA in Boston two days after coming home and again later that week. There were many trips to Boston initially. It wasn't too bad though, because it got me up and out of the house. I remember the first time I had a flashback was at my initial clinic visit after the transplant. Lee dropped me off at the front of the hospital and told me to wait in the lobby. I was wearing a mask and gloves for protection from outside germs. People were staring at me. I walked in the front door and I began to shake uncontrollably and crying. I imagine that I looked quite pathetic. The last time I walked through those doors, I was there to fight for my life. I didn't leave one room for weeks and that crap wreaks havoc on your head and I was screwed up. Lee walked in to find me crying and shaking and I'm sure he was thinking he couldn't handle another one of those days. We walked through the halls of the hospital, we reached clinic and I calmed down until.....I smelled the antibacterial gel. That was a prominent smell during my time there and all I knew was I wanted out!! I really think I may have some flight issues, because I always wanted to run. Not that I could physically run. Walking was enough of a struggle. I still have a tough time if I smell that particular antibacterial gel. I fight not to go back to the hospital days in my mind. After that experience, Lee found a side door right near the clinic so I never walked through the freaking hospital again. It made it all so much easier for me. Still crappy, but easier.

Dr EA agreed that I could see Dr Friend part of the time so I only needed to go to Boston once a week after the first couple weeks of being out of the hospital. I had to go often not only to check my blood work, but also to check my anti-rejection drug level and my liver function (LFT'S). If I had the tests in Boston, Dr EA could tell me right away if I needed to change my dosage for my meds. If I had my tests done in CT, Dr Friend had to find a specific lab to check my anti-rejection drug level and have the results sent to Dr EA who would then email me my dosage changes, as long as it wasn't anything significant. If anything was wonky, Dr EA would give me a call. This all happened at least twice a week. We had an incredible system going and it was working! We were like the three musketeers of transplant!!

My appointment in Boston on April 2nd was a good one. Dr EA said that I was progressing well and I only needed to make the trip every two weeks. Yippee!!!! He also told me that I could go to Mel's house for Easter, as long as it was just our immediate family. Double yippee!!! That may have been the best Easter ever. I wasn't able to make my usual goodies, but I was able to celebrate the first holiday with my family. The only people there were Mel, Jack, my nephew Johnny, Lee, Bill and myself. It was weird that Mel didn't have a houseful and I felt kind of bad that she couldn't have her usual friends there, but it was the most awesome Easter ever! I was only able to eat a couple forkfuls of ham and potatoes; all that mattered to me was that I was with my family. It was another day that I doubted would ever happen, but it did happen. It was another milestone in this rocky climb out of the "c" word world.

Eventually, I got up enough nerve to ask the doctor if I could go into CVS without a mask on and he said, "Sure, as long as there are no people in the store." He thought he was quite the comedian and it did make me laugh. It was a very funny way of letting me know that I needed to follow the rules. NO leaving the house without a mask and gloves. If I was outside or in the car and not in a crowd or a construction area I usually didn't wear the mask. People always stared at me with the mask on, but I didn't care. It surprised Lee that I didn't let it bother me, but the only other alternative was being a prisoner in my home. That was not appealing to me at all. I had been isolated enough.

I was not only frustrated by the thought of having to stay away from people, I was also frustrated not being able to do things for myself. Every single thing in my life had become a huge chore. I had to grocery shop online and the groceries were delivered to my house. Sounds great doesn't it? Well, it would have been awesome if I had any concept of the sizes of jars and boxes. I often thought that I was ordering a normal size of something, then when it was delivered the item looked like it belonged in a kiddie kitchen. I was not a fan of someone else picking out meat for me even though whoever was doing the shopping for me usually did a good job. Lee almost always put the groceries away…with my direction. My kitchen wasn't my own anymore. Things were not organized the way I used to have them. Everything was so different and I didn't like it at all. My logical mind told me that Lee had a lot on his plate and he was doing a really good job, but the rest of me wanted things the way they used to be. I wanted everything to be the way I wanted them to be, without any changes. I never said anything, but it was driving me insane. My life wasn't my own. It had become a stranger's life. Normal didn't exist for me any longer.

Laundry was yet another hurdle to overcome. I would go upstairs and separate the laundry and then Lee would put them in the washing machine. When they were finished he would bring me the wet clothes so I could put them on racks in the living room. When they were dry I would fold them neatly and put them back in the laundry basket, to be dispersed among the family. Putting the clothes away was a whole other difficulty. I was always so exhausted and I was still suffering from cramps in my back and that was all on top of still being very weak. I'm very particular about how my laundry is done so I'm pretty sure that I drove Lee crazy with all of my demands. I actually called my sister Mel to help get the piles of clothes in my room put away. I hated asking for help with everything. The energizer bunny's batteries had run out and recharging was taking longer than expected.

It was unbelievably annoying to be dependent on other people. I was the one who drove Bill to and from school. I was the one who went to the grocery store. I was the one who made dinner every night. I was the one who cleaned and made sure our lives ran smoothly. Then, one fateful day, I became the one who had to constantly ask my family and friends for help. I couldn't even drive a car in the beginning. My frustration level was through the roof. I wanted my life back, including all the chores and small things that make up everyone's daily routines and I wanted to be able to do those things without help. The thing I wanted to do the most was make dinner for my family. My exhaustion and pain kept me from doing that for a very long time. I remember that the first thing I made for Bill was fried wontons. I had to pull the stool over to the counter after a few minutes because it was difficult to stand at the stove for any length of time, but I did it! It was a huge accomplishment for me and I tried to do a little bit more everyday. I was going to get my life back one way or another. I was the caregiver not the other way around!

The worst part for me after transplant was that I had to go back to the Connecticut hospital for transfusions. The transfusion room was down the hall from my original room during induction and the thought of being there was beyond words. I would almost argue with Dr Friend when he would send me for a transfusion. I would beg him not to make me go even though I knew that my red blood cells were way too low. It was a large room with six or more chemo chairs on the perimeter. Each chair had its own television on one of those adjustable arms. I would always have to be pre-medicated so I had to ask Pauline to bring me if Lee was working and I've already shared my distain for pre-meds. Also, because the nurses for the transfusions were also the regular floor nurses, sometimes the wait was lengthy. It could be five or six hours in the chemo chair from beginning to end. I always thought that it was a complete waste of my day. Now you would think that the people would all chat with each other, but not at all. Some people would sleep, other people would read or watch TV, some might talk on the phone, but no chit chatting. I kind of understood, because who the hell wants to deal with strangers when you feel like crapola. There was a bathroom in the room and when someone went in there, you could hear everything! And I mean everything! I didn't like to pee in there unless I was in the big room alone and forget about pooping.

I want to stress again that this was my experience with MDS/AML and transplant. Everyone is different and the way we all react depends on many variables. Such as: age at diagnosis. How physically fit at time of diagnosis. How progressed the disease is at time of diagnosis. How close the match is. Just to name a few. I would never want anyone to be frightened by reading my story. No two of us are exactly the same and all of our body's reactions to things differ. I think that is really important to realize and emphasize.

Chapter 26
Venturing Out In Public

My first outing not to a doctor was to the furniture store. Our new couch was slowing disintegrating under our hineys. The foam was no longer springy; it was more like a pancake. I know that I spent most of my time sitting in the corner of the couch, but I was also getting skinnier every day. The store agreed to replace the faulty furniture. Lee and I made the trek forty-five minutes away to the store to pick out new furniture. As soon as we entered the parking lot I began to suit up. With the gloves and mask in place we made our way into the store. I think every single person stopped and stared at me as if I was a circus sideshow freak. The stares didn't matter to me. I was out of the hospital, I was out of the house, I was able to walk around a store and I was alive. That was all that mattered to me. I was proud of wearing the mask and gloves and wig. I had survived something that many people don't live through. So all those people could suck it!! I did tell the sales clerk why I was wearing the mask and gloves and I'm pretty sure I was the talk of the store once we left. I mean really, how often do you meet someone who just had a bone marrow transplant! I'm an anomaly and I know it. Instead of hiding from it, I've attempted to embrace this odd thing that has happened to me.

My time consisted of either doctor appointments or television for the first couple of months. I would wake up and shower, not the ritual I once had, but still a small ritual. Lee would help me put my lines in a small plastic bag and then we would cover the cross on my chest with plastic wrap and tape it all down against my skin to keep it dry and sanitary. I only used the white towels that were bleached with every use, and my bare feet still couldn't touch the ground. Lee would make me scrambled eggs some days and I would only eat about a tablespoon or so in the beginning. We learned quickly that if too much food were put on my plate, I wouldn't eat at all, so we started with very small amounts. Smaller portions seemed to work for me. I would check my medication list and take my morning dosages, but I knew there would be more meds in a couple hours. Like I've said, routines were very important for me. It was the only thing I had control over and I held on to them like a dog with a bone. It was my only sense of normalcy since my ship went off course.

At 1:00PM, Monday through Friday, I would turn on my soap opera and set up all the stuff to flush my lines. I would wash my hands, put down a paper towel, line up the alcohol wipes and syringes, and I put on the blue, non-latex gloves to begin yet another ritual. I used the alcohol wipes to disinfect the end of my line where the syringe twisted on to and I injected a certain amount and then pulled back to check for a blood return. That was a good sign that the lines were open. I did that for all three lumens or lines. I know there were a few more steps to all of that, but those are the main things that I remember. Every 72 hours, I had a visiting nurse. She came to change the dressing over the triple lumen hickman in my chest. She also would flush my lines and review things with me. I had a couple different nurses for a short time, so nothing earth shattering happened with them. I did learn about a new kitchen gadget from one of the nurses so of course I had to buy it. It was just a chopping device and I may have a small addiction to kitchen gadgets. Okay, anything kitchen related! And shoes.

Prior to leaving the hospital, I had applied for disability. The social worker and some guy from finance area told me that I would probably have to apply twice because they always reject you the first time. Well, they sure did reject me the first time. Lee called me one afternoon to tell me that the letter had arrived and I was denied disability. I was considered one hundred percent disabled, but I couldn't collect disability. I was denied because I didn't have enough quarters in the system, meaning that I hadn't worked long enough, oh, and my husband made too much money. I had raised my son and I had only been back in the work force for eighteen months before getting sick. I even checked with an attorney and she said I would only be rejected again because of not having enough quarters. This system is nonsense!! I'm being punished for raising my own child!! I also have given more to my community than the average person and doesn't that account for anything? If I had an issue and was living off of the government and never worked a day in my life, I could have collected. Where is the justice in that?!?! I'm not saying that I expected a full paycheck, but even a small percentage of what I was making when I became ill would've been great. It sucks losing so much of yourself through all this crap and then to have to go to my spouse for money makes the degradation even worse. You lose so much through the process of being ill and then not having the money to even buy a gift is really friggin annoying. I do realize that my plight is minor compared to all the people who can't pay for their meds or get the treatment they so desperately need because of all the political bullshit!! I get it, life isn't fair, but this really pisses me off!!!! End of rant!

Chapter 27
Getting Back to Normal?

Sorry for the tirade. I needed to get it off my chest. Speaking of getting something off my chest. The time had come to remove the triple lumen hickman from my chest. It came sooner than I had anticipated and Dr EA didn't think I needed it any longer. I didn't want them to take it out. I was nervous about not having it anymore. It's where all the medication, chemo and stem cells went when I was in the hospital. It saved the veins in my arms from being so painful. They weren't just lines coming out of my chest, they were my lifelines. They were also another avenue for infection, so that's why it needed it to come out as soon as Dr EA thought I was well enough and I was finally well enough. The procedure to remove the triple lumen hickman was done in an operating room. Not a big giant operating room, but a smaller more intimate environment. This meant that I needed to be prepped. UGH!

I was back in Boston for the procedure and in radiology they gave me a hospital gown to put on. I was in a small and I mean small, changing room and for the life of me, I couldn't put that hospital gown on. I sat on the little bench thing in the room and guess what? I began to cry. I know, shocking that I was crying, as if I hadn't done enough of that already.

I did not want to put that thing on ever again. In my mind, I was right back in my hospital room getting dressed after my shower. I thought, oh no not again! There was a knock on the changing room door and a nice gentleman asked me if I was almost ready and if I was okay. I had managed to put on the hospital gown and I opened the door to say I was fine. He said, "Are you sure?" I said no and began to fall apart. I explained through the tears what happened and he just comforted me until I was able to go for the biopsy. Damn, I'm crying just writing this. I think I'm overwhelmed by the compassion of a stranger. I don't always remember the kindness that was shown to me during my "c" word experience. I need to remember these things in order to remind myself how much good there is in this world.

The two men in the operating room were cheering me on and saying what an enormous feat it was to get this appendage removed so quickly after transplant. They kept congratulating me and I think they made me excited, because they were so happy for me. The twilight meds were additionally contributing to my jubilation. When I entered the operating room, I was quite dubious that removing these lines was for the best. I distinctly remembered the discomfort of bruised and abused veins and it wasn't any fun. This thing in my chest was familiar. I felt like it kept me safe. As weird as it may sound, it had become a part of me. The fighting to get healthy part of me, but it was time to move on and see the bright side. The operating room dudes won me over. I now could shower without the rigmarole of protecting the catheters. I had to look at this as one more step to freedom. The scar on my chest from the triple lumen hickman is the badge of a fighter and survivor. I wear it with pride! Most transplant survivors have the same scar, so it's almost like our own little secret handshake. I'll show you my scar if you'll show me yours. HA!

For the first one hundred days after transplant, I was lonesome. My sister Mel and a few friends would drop by regularly, but I missed being out in the world. The months of isolation were taking a toll. Not being able to touch anyone was taking a toll. Knowing that life was going on without me was taking a toll. Then came the great news that my son Bill was being awarded a very high honor in JROTC. He was going to be and still is the highest decorated cadet from his high school. The problem was that he was being given his award before my hundred days were up and I would have to wear a mask and gloves. I still had a month to go. UGH! I didn't want to wear that stuff and take any attention away from all the cadets getting their awards, so I called Dr. EA. I told him everything and he said I could go without my Halloween costume! Yippee!! But there were restrictions. No touching anyone. No eating the food. Sit away from the crowd. Avoid anyone who is coughing or sneezing. Bill's Commander accommodated my request to have a table by the door, so I wasn't in the crowd.

I was extremely proud and I couldn't wait to celebrate his accomplishment with him. It was one of those moments that made all the pain and struggle to get well absolutely worth it. I would have gone through it all over again, to be able to watch my son slowly becoming a man. Mel came from New York, so I drove with her to the event. Lee had Bill, Matt and Missy with him. While Mel and I were in the car together, she asked me if I was all right. I wasn't. I was scared to death! I hadn't been in public without protection for months. Again, here was another thing that initially freaked the hell out of me and then, being without protection, freaked the hell out of me. Unfortunately, fear was something I had become very accustomed to. I had also learned how to fight through it. I walked into the event being the proudest mom you could ever imagine. I was probably the loudest hooting and howling and whistling (you know the whistle with your fingers in your mouth) person in the room. Life was looking much different to me and every milestone was worthy of a loud whistle or two.

Chapter 28
Back to the City Council

That was the only time I was allowed to go anywhere without a mask and gloves for the one hundred days. I was back to being incognito the next day. I wanted to go to the May City Council meeting and see all my friends, so I emailed my request to Dr EA. He said okay as long as I suited up, my area was disinfected and again, no one touched me. I also needed to bring my 8:00pm meds with me and I was only allowed to stay until about 9:00pm. He stressed, not to over do it. I called the mayor and told him about my plan to attend and my friend Pauline went into the council chambers ahead of time and cleaned my area. I kept my re-emergence fairly quiet. The plan was to go directly to the Mayor's office to avoid being around the crowd as much as possible and to walk into the meeting with him at the last moment.

I was still keeping up on all the city business as much as possible over the past couple months so I would be prepared for my return. All my clothes were baggy, but I threw together something that didn't look too bad. I decided to wear my dressier wig. It was similar to my old hair, just straighter. It was a good wig, but I really hated wearing it. I don't think it fit properly. Anyway, I was ready to go and Lee decided to drive me. I entered City Hall through the front door and went directly up to the third floor where the mayor's office is. Normally, I would have entered through the side door, also called the mayor's door, but I knew all the other council members would be going in that way. I remember the mayor looking at me and saying, "Are you ready?" All I could say was "Yup." This was the first time that I had entered those chambers since that meeting when I surprised everyone all those months ago. I actually was there again. WOW!!!

We walked up the hallway, which seemed like miles and finally reached the chambers. I entered the room from the side door, walked up the two steps to the dais and sat in my seat. There was a quiet mumble in the room. I think the mask kind of threw people off a little. People were waving at me and saying hi, but I know my appearance was slightly jarring. It came time for roll call. Some of us would say "here" and others would say "present." I was a "present" person, but not that night. When my name was called out I said, "I'm baaack," and the room erupted in cheers and tears. I had only missed two meeting since transplant, but I knew there were those who questioned my ability to survive. Hell, I wasn't positive that I would survive the nightmare. I can't describe how it felt sitting there again. It was a glimpse of my old life. It was incredible to see my friends. I missed them all so much. I even missed the people who annoyed the crap out of me. It was difficult to concentrate that night. I was excited and all I could do was look at every person, chair, light, clock and microphone as if I had never seen them before. All the things that were so familiar months before were brand spankin' new in my eyes. I lasted at the meeting for about an hour or so and then exhaustion set in. I was deliriously happy. I really was back!

Truth be told, I was partially back. I would say hi to people that I knew well before the transplant and they would look at me without any recognition. Some people would be polite and say hi, but others just gave me that awkward head tilt and side smile. They had no freaking idea who I was. I suspect that between the weight loss, the wig and the fact that I was really alive, made some peeps question who was saying hello to them. Like I've said before, I don't think most people expected me to survive. I can't blame them. This whole bone marrow transplant was completely foreign to me a few months earlier. I mean, who the hell get their bone marrow decimated and then replaced and then their blood type changes. It's a little bizarre!! It was a huge struggle looking so different. Not being recognized by friends and dealing with something else new. There was too much newness in a very short time. I looked different and it was one more change I needed to learn how to deal with. It wasn't easy glancing into the mirror and not being familiar with the person who looked back.

See it wasn't just random people who didn't recognize me, I didn't recognize myself. Crazy stuff!! It took some time, but I eventually became comfortable with my new unfamiliar looks. It was freaky and sometimes when I was alone, I would shed a few tears for the old me. It's strange to grieve for yourself.

The big change came when my hair was finally long enough to take off the wig. I had stopped by the mayor's office for a small birthday party and there were maybe five to ten people sitting around the conference table eating cake. Of course, I was sipping on water, because the thought of eating cake was repulsive and one of the guys asked me what my real hair looked like. I kept telling everyone that my hair was a silver white color, but all they could picture was my long mane of different colors. I am a firm believer in changing it up often when it comes to my hair, so I had been a blonde, a brunette, a red head, a brunette with blonde highlights, a dark purple color with red highlights etc… They were all dying; get it dying, to know my real hair color. So I asked if they really wanted to know and with a resounding yes, I whipped off the wig and threw it on the conference table, never to put it on again. Everyone loved the color and to this day my hair color hasn't changed again for two reasons: 1. I really like the color and 2. I don't want to put all those chemicals on my head. Needless to say, my inch long, silver white hair, made me virtually unrecognizable. I was told that I never appeared to be sick and I believe that was true. It paid to be chubby when I got ill. It's also a fact that not very many friends saw me at my worst. I never took any photos while I was going through treatment and I kind of regret that decision now. At the time, I thought that I would NEVER want to look back on any of it. I thought that I would just move on and not think of it again. I was a silly girl!

Chapter 29
One Hundred Days

June 9, 2007 was my one hundred day mark. In transplant terms, that is huge! A holy grail of sorts. The thought being, that it takes approximately one hundred days for the transplant to be engrafted and the immune system to be better. I can't say that my immune system was great and it will always be compromised, but at day one hundred it was very much improved. I could leave the house and not be in a mask and gloves any longer!!! Incredible! I could eat fresh fruits and vegetables, no more special diet. I still wasn't eating much, so the food thing was more ceremonial than reality, but it was another step forward. One hundred freaking days behind me! First thing I needed to do was have another bone marrow biopsy to make sure that all of the nasty "c" word was gone. It was a day that I could never have imagined seven months prior. It was one hell of a long seven months. It was a time when days seemed more like months and months seemed like years. There were many days in the hospital when time moved slowly and immense sadness crept in. Day one hundred was freaking amazing! It was behind me.

Monday, June 11th was bone marrow biopsy day. It wasn't just another trip to Boston for a check up....noooo, this was going to tell us if the transplant was working. My nerves were completely on edge. I held onto my Mary medal and rubbed my fingers over the smoothness for protection and comfort. This was the time that the doctor was having a difficult time numbing my hip. I was becoming a little aggravated being stuck with all the needles and it was taking a long time, so I told the doctor to just go in for the biopsy. He was close enough to the bone and I wanted it over with already. I think Dr EA thought I was out of my mind for asking for the biopsy without complete numbing, but it was time to get it done. I grabbed onto the side of the bed and told the doctor that I was ready and to "please just do it!" Lee's face turned white and he couldn't believe what I had requested. It was over in no time and all I felt was relief. Oh, don't get me wrong, it hurt like hell, but it was over quickly. PHEW!!!

Then the waiting began. The pain was easy compared to the waiting. It seemed like forever waiting for the results of the biopsy. I am normally a fairly happy individual. I'm not usually grouchy. I was a whole different animal while I waited for biopsy results. I was quick tempered and grumpy. I was so not myself and the anxiety was tremendous. It sucks waiting to hear if you are going to live or die. I guess that could put anyone in a bad mood. At first, Lee and Billy would snap back, but when they realized what I was going through, they let me be slightly ornery. Especially since it was out of character for me to behave that way. Well, instead of hearing about the bone marrow biopsy, the doctor called and said that I needed a liver biopsy. My liver function test was high, so he suspected GVHD (graft verses host disease) in my liver. Great, just what I needed!

Monday, June 18th, back to Boston for a liver biopsy. Here we go, one more biopsy and another visit to the radiation department with the young man who called everyone "amigo", another day of having an IV stuck in my arm and another operating room. This shit was getting old. I hated all the waiting. First I waited to be called in to see the nurse, then I waited to get the IV inserted into my sorry ass veins, then I waited in the waiting room in a hospital gown and a friggin huge IV needle that hurt, until they were ready to do the biopsy. Sometimes this process took hours and my patience would be thin. I hated and I mean hated being in that waiting room. My grouchiness would turn into anger. I would tell Lee that if they didn't take me in a certain amount of time, I was leaving. He always ignored me, which was the only thing he could do. He knew I wouldn't really leave.

I think Lee was more grateful than me when they finally called me in to do the biopsy. He must have been happy not to have to listen to my mouth for a little while. I was grateful for the twilight medication. It made me nice again! The liver biopsy wasn't bad at all. They found my liver on the ultrasound and then inserted a needle to get a sample. As usual, the anticipation was the worse part. I take that back, the worse part was waiting for the nurse to take out the IV. After the procedure there was more waiting in that waiting room. They should call it the torture room. I am seeing that I have a pattern of impatience, but there is just so much anyone can take!! Patience is a virtue that I don't possess. I know this about myself.

On June 15th, I received a phone call from Dr EA. The bone marrow biopsy came back EXCELLENT!!!!!! I cried like a baby and I called everyone I knew with the incredible news. June 20th, another phone call from Dr EA, no liver GVHD!!! The cloud was lifting and I was seeing the glorious blue sky. On July 20th, the day after my forty-sixth birthday, I was told that my blood type had changed to my sister's blood type. I swear that I felt it change and I told Lee when I thought it happened. I don't know how I knew or exactly what I felt that made me think that my blood type had changed, it was just a knowing, HOLY CRAP!!!!! This news was phenomenal and creepy. As wonderful and life-saving that the news was, it was also a loss. I needed a little room to grieve. I lost a huge part of myself. It may not have been something people could see, but it was a part of me and it was gone. My identity was shaken again. I not only looked different on the outside, I was also different on the inside. The amount of different emotions I went through after that phone call is inexplicable. I was thankful beyond words that Mel was willing to donate her bone marrow. I was thrilled that the transplant was working and I was okay. I was completely freaked out that my blood type changed. I was alive and getting better every day. What a wonderful, crazy, freaky and mind-blowing miracle I experienced!!

Chapter 30
Blasted GVHD

All was quiet in my medical world until my monthly visit to Boston in August. I saw Dr Mac this time and he informed me that I needed another liver biopsy and this time they were fairly sure that I had GVHD of the liver. I was not a happy camper. Dr Mac had never seen the irritable side of me until that day and he didn't put up with my crap. I was being a baby and I tried to convince him, in my whiney voice, that I was fine. He scolded me and scheduled the liver biopsy for August 28th. Well, now you know the whole routine with radiology etc...so there's no reason for me to repeat the happenings with Mr. Amigo and the waiting that annoyed me so much. Suffice it to say, a couple days after the biopsy, I was told that I did indeed have GVHD of the liver. Some of my meds were increased and it put my vaccination schedule back quite a bit, but it wasn't bad. Livers get better and mine recovered quickly. I don't drink alcohol anymore and I'm cautious with my liver, but that is just me. I was never told that I shouldn't consume alcohol; I choose not to take the chance.

The months following the transplant were challenging at times. There was one morning that I woke up and my skin was black any place that I would sweat, like the inside of my elbows and knees, under my arms and boobs and other places, if you get my drift. I called Mel on the phone and I was basically laughing about my skin changing color. I knew that this was a possibility with the anti-rejection medication, but I had no idea to what extent. The doctor made sure that I knew that this unusual condition wouldn't last forever and I didn't need worry about another huge change in my life. I think my skin permanently changing color would have been a little more than I would have been capable of handling. Mel was laughing hysterically on the phone as I was explaining with all the dramatics that I could muster up about turning black. Then, the thought entered my mind about my nether region and how sweaty that area can become, especially in the summer. I was freaking out and yelling. I wasn't yelling in a bad way, I was yelling in an incredulous way. I told Mel that I was bringing her, on the phone, into the bathroom with me to check out the private parts. I may have screamed at the sight. Okay, I know I screamed at the sight. We were both full on belly laughing and something that could have been disturbing, ending up being another funny story of my adventures through the "c" word maze. It was just another weird thing in my ever-growing list of unusual happenings.

Another side effect of the anti-rejection drug was facial hair. Oh yeah, just what I needed was facial hair. Hey, I know I'm of Mediterranean descent, so the last thing I needed was additional facial hair! I went without any hair on my body for so long and now my face was covered with fur. Greeaat!! I was positive that my family was going to start calling me Chewy. I was tempted to buy moustache wax and just go for the handlebar look, but instead I e-mailed Dr EA. My e-mail went something like this:

Dr EA,
Not only is my skin turning black, but I'm also getting furry. Can I do something about the fur? I'm quite the sight to see!
Thanks and smooches,
MT

He said I could wax or shave. I actually don't remember how I handled the situation; it was so minor in the grand scheme of things. I do recall that my eyelashes were coming back awesome! I was so glad to have eyelashes again and they came in full and long. No more dust and cat hair in my eyes! Yippee!

I slowly began entering the world again. Lee and I would go to Wal-Mart, but for some reason, I had a hard time in there. I would start sweating and shaking and I usually had to leave and wait in the car. We began to suspect that it had something to do with the lighting. I would be okay in the beginning, but as we went around the store, I would start to feel sick. It took months for me to be able to tolerate going in there for more than ten minutes. It happened occasionally in other places, so I spent a lot of time waiting in the car for Lee.

My favorite outing had to have been going to the diner. Lee and I frequented this one diner and we became friendly with the other regulars and waitresses. I loved going to the diner on Fridays for lunch, because they had a turkey special. It was turkey, gravy, stuffing, mashed potatoes and cranberry sauce. I love turkey! I know Pauline kept the diner people informed of my progress. She had been a great source of support through my illness and she enjoyed bragging about how far I had come. When I was finally allowed to eat somewhere other than my home and my appetite was back a little, Lee and I went to the diner for turkey. Pauline met us there and I think she was as excited as I was to be enjoying something normal. Our favorite waitress, Voula, came right over to us and I was so happy to see her. She knew immediately that I was there to have my turkey. For most people having the turkey special at a diner isn't a big deal, but it was something I had been looking forward to. I was finally doing something that I enjoyed. I didn't have to look for a silver lining or change my perspective to make it tolerable. It made me happy and I loved the turkey special for what it was, a turkey special.

Chapter 31
Re-election Time

In July of 2007, I was nominated by my party to run for my third term for the City Council. I was determined to do it and win. I spoke to both of my doctors about running for election while still recovering. One doctor didn't think that it was a great idea, but the other one said he thought it was all right. Of course, I listened to the one who said what I wanted to hear and I accepted the nomination. I had so much doubt. I didn't have all my strength back. I still wasn't eating very much. And my immune system was on the mend. People promised to help me campaign, but we all know how that goes. I was pretty much on my own. It sucks knocking on doors, but I knew that all the walking was very good for me. I also avoided touching people as much as possible. Germs were not my friends.

Nominations for the City Council were on my birthday. I thought, what a great way to celebrate and have many of my friends around me. This was also the night I saw my friend, Art, for the first time since he was diagnosed with the same thing as me. Art called me in February, when I was in between hospitals, to tell me that he just found out that he had MDS that turned into AML. Art is a more mature man and his struggles were very different then mine, but we bonded over our mutual disease. We had worked on the State Rep. campaign together. What the hell are the chances that two of us came down with the exact same thing? At this time Art was preparing for his transplant in August in New York. Just like me, his sister was his match. Not only did his blood type change, so did his chromosomes. He is now XX verses XY. I know, this is some crazy stuff! Anyway, Art was in mask and gloves and when I saw him, I ran right over. We hugged each other, which was against the rules for both of us, and I cried. Yes, I cried again. They had us both dead, but we showed them up!! HA! This was actually the moment that the elbow bump was born. Neither Art nor myself could touch people's hands. Way too many germs!!! We raised our elbows to bump each other instead of touching hands. It became a thing and it caught on quickly. Everyone knew that when they greeted Art, or myself that they had to raise their elbows and not put out their hands. It worked for us.

Sometimes not shaking hands could be uncomfortable especially when someone wasn't aware of my medical history. There was an event where paratroopers were landing in a field to honor a group of Veterans. The Lieutenant Governor was attending and I was introduced to him. As he put out his hand to shake mine, I crossed my arms in front of myself, so he wouldn't touch me. What an awkward moment!!! With that, the person who was introducing us leaned into the Lieutenant Governor and whispered in his ear why I reacted the way that I did. He smiled at me and nodded his head. I'm pretty sure that his initial reaction was, what a rude bitch! I wanted to scream, "I'm honestly not a rude bitch, you just have germs that could make me sick!" Even though I knew that there was nothing that I could have done about the situation, I was a little embarrassed. After that uncomfortable introduction, I headed back out of the crowd to sit under a tree with Lee. It was safer there.

Safety became something I cherished. Feeling unsafe and out of control had become a way of life. As much as I tried to make things feel normal through routine, nothing felt normal or safe anymore. Nothing should feel more safe than the touch of people you love and that had been taken away months ago. I had always loved being around people and suddenly I feared them. All people were a threat to my health. After all these years, the sound of someone coughing near me freaks me out and I think I've made Lee a little paranoid about it too. I will move as far away from them as is humanly possible, oh and reasonable. I also really love little kids, but they are the biggest threat of all. I know, I know, I have issues. I used to let kids sit on my lap and play with them, but now that doesn't happen often anymore. I've gotten a little better about it recently. I just wash my hands, use antibacterial gel and change my clothes as soon as I get home. Maybe I'm just mildly neurotic now.

Then there is the mall. Which in my opinion is the biggest germ bowl in the world, especially the food court. There are just way too many banisters, people, and things that too many strangers touch. It makes me feel uncomfortable. They touch everything. Clothes, earrings, shoes, display cases, makeup, kitchen items etc... just everything!!! It's so germ infested! I try not to go to the mall during flu season. There are too many unknown things flying through the air. Oh and they keep the mall so damn hot that I just know that all the bad stuff is breeding rapidly. Then there are public bathrooms. I hate them, enough said! I'm completely grossing myself out. UGH!

Chapter 32
Getting Involved

Somewhere in the month of August or so, I went to a meeting for the Leukemia and Lymphoma Society (LLS) walk. My friend who is a lymphoma survivor invited me to tag along with her. I was able to meet the parents of a child who was surviving leukemia and a few other survivors, but it was too much for me. I wasn't ready to get involved on that level yet. I was still trying to get myself in order and I felt overwhelmed. I wasn't ready for that type of commitment to an organization at the time. The woman from LLS, Danny, was so kind to me and I think she knew it was a little more than I could handle. I did make her touch my hair because it was so soft and I thought that it felt like puppy fur. Four years later when I was finally able to become involved with LLS, Danny remembered me as the person who made her touch my hair. Geez, what an odd thing to be remembered for! She must have thought that I was very strange. She wasn't too far off base.

While I was at home recovering and spending most of my time in front of the TV, it dawned on me that I really needed to do something positive. Although I had been going through all of this ickyness, I also knew that I was one of the lucky ones. I was one of the thirty percent of the people with a sibling match. I thought about all of the people who didn't have a match and how frightened they must be. I knew the fear. I felt it while I waited to hear if one of my sisters was my match. I wondered what would have happened to me if I didn't have a match. The fear of the unknown is indescribable. Maybe it's not fear of the unknown; maybe it's just the fear of death. Either way fear can swallow you up and the thought of so many people feeling like that, encouraged me to do my part. I decided that I was going to organize a bone marrow drive. It wasn't like being completely thrown into an organization; I could do this on my own and at my own pace.

So it began. Many phone calls were made trying to figure this thing out. I finally got in touch with "Be the Match", an organization that swabs people to go onto the National Bone Marrow Registry. At the time, the person or organization running the drive had to come up with the cost of the swabbing for each person. I'll admit, I'm not much of a fundraiser so I called my friend Art. Remember, Art was the other person who was diagnosed with MDS/AML and he said that he would help. Art called a couple friends of his from out of state and they covered the cost of the initial testing for me!! So the money was taken care of. Now I needed a location. It should have an area for people to sit at a table and fill out paperwork. I thought there should be separate area with some cookies and treats as a way of thanking those people who were willing to go onto the registry and possibly save a life. I knew of the perfect location, city hall. I called up the mayor and he said of course I could do it there. I mean come on, was he really going to say no to me? Actually the mayor never said no to me when I asked him about stuff like this. I think he may now fear when I call him and say, "I have an idea!" I'm actually quite surprised he still takes my calls.

Money, check. Location, check. "Be the Match" attending, check. Next step, getting the people there. I knew that was going to be the hardest part of all. It's scary. This whole bone marrow stem cell stuff is scary. All most people have ever heard of is how painful it is to have the needles stuck in your hip for a bone marrow aspiration and the average person really fears pain. So I knew I needed to educate people. The public needed to know that the transplant is usually stem cells. Not the controversial stem cells, but consenting adult stem cells. They needed to know that the initial test is a cheek swab. I knew that the best way to do that was to put a face and story with the disease and treatment. I sent out a press release about my story. The newspaper picked it up and made my story their Monday morning profile. The photographer came to my house to take pictures in all different poses. The pose that ended up on the front page of the paper was me lying on my stomach, on our green and white hammock with my hand under my chin. We call it the cheesecake photo. Actually, it may be my favorite picture of myself that anyone has ever taken. I'm not very photogenic, so a good picture is a gift. The story did draw some attention.

Chapter 33
Public Speaking

Another way that I attempted to spread the word was that I contacted all of the service organizations in my area and asked if I could go to their meeting and share my story. At the time, the thought of speaking in front of people made me a nervous wreck. I always had to pee just before it was time to speak and I usually didn't have time. I probably didn't really have to pee, it was my body being nervous. Just before I would be introduced, I would feel a sinking feeling in the pit of my stomach. In the beginning, my hands would shake uncontrollably and my voice would tremble. I occasionally still have a little tremble in my voice at the beginning of speaking to groups about being ill. It's very personal. I also think it's a responsibility to know the audience and not say things to frighten the listener, especially if there are children present. Other audiences have to be hit right between their eyes with the severity of this process. I learned through speaking to those groups that each group has its own personality. Some were more receptive than others, but all in all, I felt like some people were educated about bone marrow transplants and stem cell transplants. The one thing that ALWAYS gets a reaction is when I say that my blood type changed. There is usually a gasp. That is very often the first thing people ask me about after I speak.

I went from B positive to A positive or **Be Positive to A Plus**!

One group that I spoke to was the Ladies Auxiliary of the Ancient Order of the Hibernians. I knew some of the members, which made it even more difficult. I also used to read the "Thank You" poem that I wrote to my sister, at the end of each talk.

THANK YOU

How do I thank you?
What can I say?
You've given me the chance,
To live another day.

When I found out I was sick,
And enveloped with fear,
We were told you were my match,
Your dedication was clear.

You didn't ask about pain or
How this would affect you,
You cried along with me and said,
"Now what do we do?"

Every test we went through,
You did it with pride.
You have no idea what this meant to me,
Having you by my side.

Because of you:
I can wake up every day and
Celebrate the smallest thing,
Like the wind on my face
Or to hear a bird sing.

I will be able to see my son
Leave high school and graduate.
I will be at his wedding,
When he finds his true mate.

I will dance, I will sing,
I will be the best me I can be,
Because I'm living my life now
For you too, not just me.

I hope I explained a little bit
How I feel,
But you are the one who
Made it all real.

I pray and I pray and
I thank God every night,
For you being with me always,
As my white healing light.

This was originally written as part of a local
newspaper article. The editor had approached me and
asked me to write something about my illness and I
suggested that I write something for my sister. My

poems may not always be the best and I know that I'm no e.e. cummings, but it's how I like to express myself sometimes. This one came straight from my heart. I didn't tell Mel anything about the poem; I just mailed her the newspaper with a note to tell her to look at a certain page. She called me crying.

Sometimes when I would read it to a group, it would evoke tears. It was still so fresh and new for me. I had only had the transplant five or six months earlier. I was still coming to terms with everything. My emotions were all over the place and it showed. A lovely woman with long blonde hair named Debbie asked for my number. She was kind of an organizer for an AARP group and asked if I would speak to them. Debbie said that even though they were too mature to register for bone marrow donation, they would love to hear the story. I said I would be happy to meet with them. I figured if nothing else, they could share the information with their family and friends.

It was a sunny fall day and I distinctly remember wearing gray pants, a white and blue striped button down shirt and a cobalt blue v-neck sweater when I went to meet with the AARP group. A little known fact about me is that I can be quite shy especially with people I don't know. I get very quiet and keep to myself so you can imagine how I was out of my comfort zone quite often during this time. The only person I knew was Debbie and I had only met her briefly one time. To my surprise and delight everyone was extremely friendly and they made me feel right at home. Maybe it was my white hair. I gave them my whole sordid story and here is the amazing part, they passed the hat and gave me money for the bone marrow drive. I mean, holy crow! It was seriously the most touching and thoughtful thing in the world. This group of generous people knew that they couldn't be a part of the registry, so they gave me money. I never asked for money, they just did it! It still touches me thinking about it. And if that wasn't enough, one of the gentlemen there made his granddaughter come to the drive and register. Amazing!

I received many comments about the article in the paper about the bone marrow drive. The article explained that the initial testing was nothing more then a swab of your cheek. It was very important that the public realized that there is nothing invasive about getting into the registry and possibly saving someone's life. All it is is a cheek swab. It was also important that when I spoke to people that if they weren't really willing to be a donor if called up, then they shouldn't do it at all. There is nothing worse than a person in need of a transplant believing that their life has been saved and the donor backs out. I've seen it happen and it totally and completely sucks! I lost a friend because his sibling was a perfect match and backed out. I can't imagine, I just can't imagine!!! I also have friends who are on the registry to be a donor, have gotten a call and with further testing were told that someone else was a better match and they were disappointed that they weren't able to help a stranger. I guess as rotten as some people can be, there are more people willing to put themselves out there for another person. Or at least I really hope that is the case.

One day shortly after the article was in the paper; I received a message on the answering machine from a sobbing woman. Her sister was waiting for a bone marrow match. When I returned the phone call, this poor woman was absolutely beside herself with fear and grief. It put into perspective for me what my own sisters and family had to have been battling with for all these months. UGH, what a damn nightmare for everyone involved. Sometimes as the patient it's good to be reminded that it's not all about you all the time. Other people are suffering right along with you. This woman was definitely suffering right along with her sister. The woman from the answering machine, her husband and her brother-in-law all came to the bone marrow drive and thanked me for what I was doing. She asked me if I would be willing to go to her house and meet her sister. Of course, I said yes. I walked into their house on a Wednesday evening and to my surprise there was my picture from the newspaper on the refrigerator. Geez, I didn't know what I could do or why I was really there. I'm not sure that I handled it properly. I never heard from any of them after that night. The sister who was ill wasn't doing well at all and I'm not sure that she survived. I hope and pray that she did survive. I had a lot to learn about being a survivor. Actually, at that point I wasn't positive that I would be a long-term survivor. I was still recovering and I hope that I didn't say something stupid or insensitive. It still bothers me when I think about it.

The bone marrow drive was a success! We signed up fifty-six new people for the bone marrow registry. There were friends and family of friends and my sister Mel was there to answer questions for people who were a little fearful. Also, one of the female firefighters is a leukemia survivor and she let all the firefighters know about the drive and many men in uniform showed up to register. Another bone marrow transplant survivor showed up to offer support. She was another phone call that I received because of the newspaper. It was awesome to meet another survivor and her husband. If I recall properly, I think the drive was four hours long and my ankles blew up like balloons. It was one of the side effects of one of my medications, but I didn't care. It was a great day. Tiring, but great!

Chapter 34
The Campaign

Besides working on the bone marrow drive, I was also running for re-election. My picture in the brochure that we hand out when we meet constituents had me in my good wig. My palm card, the card I handed out at the doors was a picture of me with very short white/silver hair. Some people asked if the wig picture was an old photo. Grrr! I would just smile and say that it was taken a month ago and I needed a change. I usually didn't get into the whole wig, being sick crap. There may have been a couple instances when I would talk about it, but only if the subject was appropriate. It's amazing what some people will discuss with you when you knock on their door. I was tired ninety-nine percent of the time, so I didn't push it. I learned to listen to my body. It seemed like if I let myself get over tired or worn down, I would get sick. I took it easy and I didn't campaign like I had the previous terms. I was nervous during that entire campaign. Okay, I was always nervous during campaign season, but that time was different. I needed to win verses wanting to win.

There was one day of campaigning that sticks out vividly in my mind. It was a beautiful, cool fall day and the leaves on the trees were an amazing kaleidoscope of colors. I decided to campaign on a street that was an easy walk and the homes were fairly close together. That made it much easier for me especially since I was knocking on doors alone. The candidates were encouraged not to cut across on people's lawns for a couple reasons. Number one, it's rude and number two, dog poop. Hahaha, number two...dog poop. Anyway, the air was crisp and it was becoming quite breezy. Suddenly, there was a forceful gust of wind and I stopped dead in my tracks in the middle of the road. I lifted my face up toward the sun and I felt the wonderful air on my face and I felt the movement of every leaf as the wind surrounded my body. I recalled all the time stuck in hospital rooms and how I longed for fresh air. How I wanted to be out in the world. How I dreamt of doing normal things again. I had made it. Against all odds, I had survived. I may have, at that moment looked like a crazy person to an observer, but I didn't care what anyone thought. I was privately celebrating my life. I was in my own world of amazement and gratitude as a couple of chilly tears were being brushed off my face by the breeze. It was incredible!!

Election day was cold and rainy. I woke up at four-thirty so I could be showered and ready to be at the polls when they opened. I had bought a new pair of black boots with a small heel and some fur around the ankle, in anticipation of it being a chilly election day. I was wearing a teal turtleneck, blue dress pants and a reversible coat. One side of the coat was brown fur and the other side was a black waterproof material. I loaded the pockets with gloves, knowing that they were going to get wet, so I would need backup. I was all bundled up and ready to go. I wasn't especially confident and that year I hadn't campaigned like I had in previous years. It concerned me. I always felt like you never know what someone is really going to do in the voting booth. It was nerve wracking!

I found my usual spot, more than fifty feet away from the polls, to set up. There are rules at the voting places. No campaigning within fifty feet of the polling place. No stickers, palm cards or any campaign material in the polling location. Yard signs must be held and not placed in the ground. Of course my rule was I needed a huge cup of coffee near me at all times. Election Day is one long ass day...and night. I placed my coffee near a tree, put up my hood, put on my first pair of gloves, picked up my sign and watched the sun rise over the nearby homes. There is something surreal standing there encouraging people to vote for you. I said good morning to the voters, but I never wanted to make anyone uncomfortable. I don't like it when anyone does that to me so I tried to be very careful. Many people would put their heads down, so they wouldn't make eye contact and I understood. I have to admit that on occasion it would make me a little paranoid because I would think that they wouldn't look at me because they didn't like me or they didn't vote for me.

There is a little known fact about candidates on election day, at least locally and that is that we call or text each other all day long. There are many phone calls from friends and family wishing the candidate luck. We also check to see how things are going at other polling places. Certain people vote early in the morning, other groups are late voters and the weather can have an affect on voter turn out. So many variables, but always an exciting day! My cell phone started ringing early this particular election day. Many other candidates for the City Council were calling to wish me luck especially with the transplant and everything. No one could believe that I was standing at the polls, alone, in the rain. A few people actually scolded me on the phone and told me to go home, but I refused. I felt like people needed to see that I was okay. I had to prove to myself that I was okay and I could do the things I used to do. I also had no intention of staying there all day. Lee was supposed to come to relieve me and my running partner would hopefully be there around noon.

I think I got home a little after noon and the first thing I did was change my socks. My feet were wet and freezing! Then, I took a nap. I was shocked that I was actually able to sleep on Election Day, but my body had had enough. I woke up and I had to get dressed again so I could head over to headquarters to make phone calls. This time I got a little more dressed up. I still wore the teal turtleneck, a navy blue skirt, brown tights, a brown tweed blazer and brown warm comfy boots. At one point that night, I got pissed because someone told me that I was losing in the absentee ballots. That's a big deal because I never lost in absentees. It was actually a ploy to get me to make more phone calls and it made me so angry, that I went to my car and cried. Honestly, it was a really mean thing to do to me and I didn't lose the absentees. It was bullshit. I began to really think that I was going to lose. The person who told me that lie, lost all of my respect that night. I was in a fragile state to begin with and still recovering from a significant illness. It was just mean! After that night, the only phone calls I would make on Election night was to people I knew and when I finished that, I fake called. I would point to the list and make believe I was speaking to someone, especially if the "powers that be" were near.

The results began to trickle in between eight and nine o'clock. The tension was building in the room and you could almost feel the electricity as everyone was waiting in anticipation of the results. I still thought that I might have lost. Thank goodness that the results for ward 7 (my ward) came in first, before I had a friggin heart attack. I won!!! I yelled out a huge WOOHOO, leapt off of my feet, hugged Lee and became teary. Holy shit!! My friend, Michael, just recently said to me how amazing it was that in less than one year, I was diagnosed with MDS/AML, spent months in hospitals, had a bone marrow transplant, was in one form of isolation or another for over four months, ran for re-election, won my seat and was starting again. PHEW! My tears were that of disbelief. I was proud of myself. I was grateful. I was going to sit in my seat on the dais for another two years. I won two more elections after that and I served a total of ten years.

The election, the rain and all the excitement definitely kicked my ass. The week after Election Day, I came down with a cold. I was still seeing Dr Friend once a week or once every other week so I figured that he would tell me that I just had a little cold and that would be the end of it. Just like when I would get a cold when I was young and it would run its course in a week or so. Yeah, that's not what happened. When I saw Dr Friend I couldn't even hear because my head was so congested and I was running a slight fever so my white blood cell count was up. Normally that wouldn't be a cause for concern, but only being a few months out from transplant made it a giant deal. I had to go to an ear, nose and throat specialist and have a chest x-ray.

My regular ENT wasn't available so I had to see a different doctor in the practice. This doctor had seen Bill a couple times, so I knew he was good. He checked me out with all those instruments looking in my throat and that metal thing up my nose etc... I could tell that this doctor was a little uncomfortable caring for me with my recent medical history so he called Dr Friend. Together they decided to put me on an antibiotic, which was also a chore because I not only had my drug allergies, but I probably had my sister's drug allergies, too. Somehow they figured it all out. I asked when I would get my hearing back to normal and the doctor said that it might be a little while. He wasn't kidding either. I went to a Council meeting and literally didn't hear anything that was being said. I didn't start feeling better for about six weeks and that is when I realized that things were never going to be the same. There will never be such a thing as a simple cold or ear infection. Little illnesses can become significant very quickly. I needed to be on my toes at all times, making my neurosis worse. I was sick and tired of being sick and tired! This was also the beginning of knowing that most doctors don't know very much about bone marrow transplants and the residual effects on the body.

Chapter 35
The One Year Mark

Christmas 2007 was both magical and scary. Once I finally recovered from the cold and subsequent infections, I was raring to go for Christmas. I had learned my lesson about not overdoing it and if I wore myself out, I could get sick, so I had to learn how to pace myself. Starting my days at six in the morning, running all day and ending at ten o'clock at night was a thing of the past. One big thing a day was good enough. I would either bake or Christmas shop on any given day, but I wouldn't do both. Everything was very slow going. I didn't make as many cookies as I normally would have made and I pared down just about everything that year. I was excited that I didn't have the threat of hospitalization looming over my head every day and I tried to enjoy every moment of the process that are the holidays. I was home and I survived to see another Christmas.

Where there should have only been sugarplums dancing in my head, there were terrible memories. I struggled through every anniversary of diagnosis, biopsy, second and third opinions and all those pesky feelings associated with those days. I would have moments of deep sadness. I cried alone. I knew no one would understand. They all just wanted me to be okay and I should have been only joyful. On certain dates, I absolutely relived the dreadful memories of the previous year. It was like nothing I had ever felt before. I was out of my mind elated to be celebrating Christmas and I was out of mind in distress over the memories. The whole thing was a contradiction. I had nowhere to turn, so I put on a happy face and focused on the positive as much as possible. I became very good at pretending.

The first year after the transplant was mostly trial and error. I knew not to get run down. If I had a lot to do for two days in a row it usually meant a couple days of recovery. The toughest lesson to learn was to listen to my body. I learned that there is transplant tired and regular tired. Regular tired meant and still means to rest. I know that if I don't rest when my body tells me to, I will feel yucky and possibly get sick. Transplant fatigue is a thing that I suffer from and it can really make me angry at times. I can usually push through it, but sometimes it kicks my butt. Exhaustion was a huge part of the theme the first year, now it's just a part of my life. Annoying, but it sure beats the alternative of pushing up daisies.

There were also side effects from my medications. One of the meds would make my ankles blow up if I were on my feet too long. I always had to carry a lunch box with me with my medications with me. I found that out the hard way one day. Lee and I went out of town for the day and I thought we would be back in time for my scheduled anti-rejection meds, but we got stuck in traffic. That was the one that had to be taken every twelve hour to keep the level of the medication in my system steady. I also needed my antibiotic to protect me from infection. I was freaking out in the car and getting very upset about not taking my meds on time. I may have sobbed slightly. After that, I always had my medications with me. It's kind of like bringing an extra pair of underwear on vacation. You never know where you can get stuck so it's best to be prepared.

I'm not going to lie, that first year and four months were sheer hell!! I never thought that I had it in me to endure so much physical and emotional pain. I never imagined that I would have to. Even writing this now it sometimes seems like it was someone else's life. I have to remind myself that it wasn't or isn't a Hallmark movie. I know I lived all of it and yet it doesn't feel like it happened to me, but then again, it absolutely feels like it happened to me. It's crazy! No matter how I felt about this crap, I knew that I was going to celebrate the first anniversary/birthday of my transplant on March 1st 2008. I made it through the first year and that was a giant step in the right direction.

As the one-year mark approached, Lee and I decided to have a party. The party wasn't anything extravagant, just pizza, salad and dessert at a local restaurant. I invited all of my family, friends, the entire City Council with spouses, the mayor, and my other friends from the city who had been such a great support for me through the rough times. Oh, I also invited my two main doctors. Dr EA couldn't make the trip from Boston, but Dr Friend was able to attend. The guest list topped one hundred people, many of who traveled from out of town. My sister Marlene from Syracuse, Mel and Jack from Poughkeepsie, Jimmy and Justine from Boston, my niece Meredith from college, and Matt and MaryBeth from Mystic.

The party was held on a Saturday afternoon. I had little flower candy dishes filled with jellybeans on each table and two tables pushed together for the cookies and treats (caramel and chocolate covered pretzels) that I had made. We knew the owner of the restaurant, so he allowed me to bring my own baked goods. I figured that it had been a long time since I had baked for anyone, so this was a small gesture of thanks. We also had a karaoke machine, which ultimately was used only to play music. I guess a Saturday afternoon isn't the ideal time for karaoke. Not enough booze flowing.

I had bought a new sweater for the occasion. It was black with bright colored polka dots. It reminded me of confetti, so I referred to the sweater as my "celebration" sweater. I was still thin and I had kept my silver hair short, so I felt quite sassy that day. My friends with the karaoke machine were the first to arrive followed by Dr Friend. The people were trickling in and I had a terrible fear that very few people would show up. I hate that feeling of dread, when you think your event is a bust. It wasn't a bust!! It was awesome!! I thanked everyone for their love and support and I told them to, "Eat, drink and be merry...oh wait I'm Mary." I really hope none of you are booing and hissing at my bad joke, at least my guests at the party chuckled. I believe that a fun time was had by all.

The only slight damper on the party was the anticipation of the one-year biopsy that I had to have in a few days. Some people thought that I shouldn't have celebrated until after I received the results, that it could be bad luck, but I wanted the party as close to the actual transplant date as possible. I still survived one year regardless of the outcome of the test. I didn't want to think about being afraid again. I was so tired of living in fear. I still am kind of sick of it. A party was just the thing to keep me grounded. It kept that horrendous, heart stopping, sick to my stomach, can't catch my breath feeling at bay, if only for a short time. The inevitable "holy shit" was coming soon enough. The biopsy was happening and I felt like this one was the true test of transplant success. No one said that to me, it was what I felt in my gut.

Here we go, another trek to Boston for another blasted test. Well maybe that's a tiny bit harsh. Part of me was looking forward to hearing something good and part of me feared hearing something bad. The biopsy itself was no big deal to me anymore and I hadn't seen Dr EA in some time. I knew my way around clinic and Lee had his parking routine down pat. He would drop me off at the side door, park the car and meet me inside. It was my home away from home, with a little pain injected for good measure. Lee and I were waiting in the examination room for the doctor when I said to Lee, "It smells like ocean in here." He mocked me and said, "Ocean? What the heck does ocean smell like?" I said, "You know, it smells like it does at the ocean." We were kind of laughing and teasing back and forth as I kept insisting that it smelled like ocean. After a few minutes my nurse came in the room and she said, "It smells like ocean in here." We burst out laughing and asked if she had been listening to us. She said no, so I told her how I had just said the exact same thing. It was very weird and the room absolutely smelled like ocean. I told Dr EA the about the aroma when he came into the room and he said he didn't smell anything. Hogwash! I was half expecting a seagull to swoop down and try to take part of Lee's sandwich. By the way, I smelled ocean before the pre-medication.

Speaking of pre-medication, I forgot to take my pain medication before the bone marrow biopsy, so I had to take liquid morphine. I don't know if I've said this before, but I really, really hate morphine. It makes me feel icky, but I guess it was better than being uncomfortable. So here we go again, another biopsy. I'm not going to bore with all details again of the workings of a biopsy, but suffice it to say, that the doctor was unable to aspirate a sample from my right side and I was getting nauseous from the morphine so we stopped after a while. I was given some anti-nausea medication and Dr EA and I discussed what to do next. I needed to have this biopsy and I needed to know that I was free of leukemia and MDS!! There was no question in my mind. I told him to do another biopsy, this time on the left side. He tried to convince me to come back and have it done in the operating room. I said that there was no way that I was leaving without a biopsy. I couldn't wait any longer to find out if I was okay, so we went ahead with biopsy number two. This one was successful! Yippee! There was one thing; Dr EA told me that the next biopsy would have to be done in the operating room. Damn it!! It was too difficult to continue to do them in an examination room, because of my weird anatomy and he felt like it was getting to be too much for me.

This is when the real torture began...waiting for the results of the biopsy. It was like watching toxic paint dry. Life entered an exceptionally slow realm of time. Tick tock, tick tock. That's all I could hear in my head. It was nearly impossible to concentrate on anything. Even watching my favorite TV show, which usually flew by, had become a mind wandering experience. I wasn't present and like before, I was a little grouchy. I would tend to get like that when I wasn't sure of my survival. It really is a horrendous feeling. I don't like waiting to find out if I could possible be sick again. It reminds me of being in a constant state of slow motion, underwater. Everything is muffled and not clear and you are unable to breath. Yucky!

Lee and I decided to try to take our minds off of all this nonsense, so we went car shopping. I had seen a commercial with a beautiful woman driving a red Cadillac, so I had mentioned to Lee how much I would like a red Cadillac...some day. We had been driving around and just pricing them, but they were way out of my budget. We stopped at a used car dealer who we had gone to a couple times previously. He had some good deals and he was unbelievably honest. To our surprise, sitting in the lot was a light blue Cadillac. Not the red that I had wanted, but this unusual blue that changes colors according to how the light hits it. Lee wanted to stop in to talk to the guy, but I was convinced that there was no way this was ever going to happen.

The dealer was a tall lanky gentleman with a very calm disposition. He told us that a GM executive had driven the car and that's why there was only eleven thousand miles on the car. There is also the fact that once a car is used, the price goes way down. I'm going to backtrack a little here and remind you that I had just had two bone marrow biopsies done the previous day. Normally, after a biopsy, I could shift my weight to one side of my hiney, so I wouldn't be directly leaning on the biopsy sight when I sat down. This time was different. There was no way to shift my weight to a good spot and I was uncomfortable. I gave up and I stood up as the guy was talking to us. I still wasn't sure about the car. I needed time to think about it, even though the price was phenomenal. This was a great diversion from all the crap. I would think about this car instead of thinking about the dreaded diseases and myself. I was so sick of myself!

After what felt like an eternity, my biopsy results came back with no evidence of disease. I cried. I always cry after I get nerve-racking test results. It's a release of the stress. I was able to think again. I wanted to celebrate, maybe with a new car? Actually, all I really wanted to do was tell my family and friends and hang out at home with Lee and Billy. It never failed; that my life felt different once my tests results came in. I was reminded of the small, wonderful things in my life and my perspective changed a little with every clean biopsy. I try to remember those feelings and not let the lessons that I learned through the bull crap go by the wayside. Oh, and I did buy the Cadillac, which may have earned me the nickname, T-money. If only that was accurate.

Chapter 36
Year Two

The second year after the transplant was the year of catching up on other doctor's appointments. The eye doctor was important because chemo can do a job on your eyes. My sisters insist that my eyes got worse due to my age, but that's a load of malarkey. At least that's my story and I'm sticking to it. Seriously though, I do suffer from dry eyes since the transplant and it can get to be quite painful. One time it got so bad, I had tiny scratches on my corneas from blinking. Crazy, right? It was nothing that a few eye drops didn't take care of. I do use a nonprescription eye drop almost daily to keep my eyes moisturized especially after a shower. The next appointment for year two was the dreaded gyno. Every woman hates and I mean hates the yearly exam. We actually talk to each other about how much we hate that appointment and we tell each other that it will all be over soon. We say things like, "This time tomorrow, it will be all done for another year." It's awful and to top it all off, the nurse weighs you. I'm sighing just at the thought of it all.

My last bone marrow biopsy took place in March. 2009. And yes, it did take place in an operating room. I swear, I think I saw every single operating room in the Boston hospital. Of course I'm exaggerating, because I suspect that there are tons of operating rooms in a metropolitan hospital, but I did spend more time in them than I ever imagined. I got to see my buddy who called everyone "amigo". It was interesting how a word that drove me crazy on my first visit had become a source of comfort and familiarity. The biopsy was like all the others except I wasn't awake. I'm not a fan of being put under, because I can get a little nauseous from the drugs. It's kind of funny that that makes me sick, but I didn't throw up from chemo. Sometimes even I think that I'm a weirdo. I went through the normal recovery room stuff. You know, the nurses saying your name and trying to wake you up and trying to get you to eat toast. Oops, I actually think they gave me a box lunch and then Lee came in to keep me company and he ate my food. Once they took the IV out of my arm, I was allowed to leave.

Lee and I were on our way home from Boston when the horrible, sick to my stomach feeling started. I was opening the window, trying to get some fresh air and I thought I was going to pass out. It was terrible. To top it all off, I had forgotten to wear sweat pants and I wore jeans to the biopsy, so the nurse gave me a pair of oversized scrub pants to wear home. Jeans are not comfortable on a fresh biopsy sight. I also wore sneakers instead of slip on shoes. I don't know what the hell I was thinking. I knew how to dress for a biopsy. I had a momentary lapse in judgment.

Anyway, I was feeling yucky. I begged Lee to please stop at the next rest area, so I could go to the bathroom. I didn't want to barf in a public restroom, so I was praying for pooping instead. Not that I like pooping in public, but it was better than having my face near a nasty toilet.

So, at the first rest area we saw, we stopped. A sense of relief came over me. I asked Lee to get me a pretzel, hoping that it would help absorb all the operating room medication. As I proceeded to get out of the car, Lee started laughing at me and told me that I looked like I escaped from a mental hospital. My top and hooded sweatshirt were all disheveled, I was wearing giant light blue hospital pants, my sneakers were untied, my hair was a mess from laying on an operating table and my skin had a gentle green hue. I also was shuffling along because the anesthesia hadn't worn off yet. I don't think that I was amused at the time and I said something like, "I don't give a shit." All I wanted to do was get to the long awaited bathroom. The fresh air and the walk from the car to the potty helped to clear my head, so the spins subsided. Needless to say, there was a very successful poop involved and no barf. I shuffled back to the car, slumped into my seat and nibbled on the pretzel on our way home.

That night we ordered Chinese food with Mel who came to our house and took care of the dogs for us;

we had gotten two Siberian Huskies along the way. It was definitely nice to have my sister at my house when we got home, even though I think the sight of me may have startled her a little. Once I ate, I felt a lot better and the greenish hue began to fade. You may be wondering why Bill didn't take care of the dogs. Well, he was at military basic training. It was brutal not having him home and I knew that he was worrying about my health. It had been very rough couple years for all of us. I was super irritable waiting for the biopsy results and having him away from home wasn't helping much. We could only talk to Bill once a week, if that often, and the stress was building. The results came back with no evidence of disease and Dr EA told me that would be my last biopsy, unless something was to show up in my blood work. He also told me that if I ever did need another biopsy, he would consider doing it in my sternum. That's the bone going down the middle of my chest and HELL NO!

Then there was the series of vaccinations that took about two years to complete. When my bone marrow was wiped out so were all of my immunizations. I had a brand new immune system, so I had to start from scratch. My Boston doctor gave my Connecticut doctor and myself a schedule to follow. I was still seeing Dr Friend every two months at that point, so it wasn't a pain in the neck or an additional appointment, we just re-immunized at my blood check-ups. For those of you who have children, I'm sure you remember the appointments for the little ones to get their shots and how for certain shots you were told to give the toddler Tylenol when you got home. Well, that is no lie!! There were one or two shots in a series that made my arm swell and honestly it made my feel like dookey. I felt so bad for the babies who had to get those shots. Wait; maybe I was acting like a baby. Well I did have to go through the immunizations twice.

All I knew was that I wanted get my immunizations over with and have my body be safe from the diseases once again. The only vaccination I couldn't receive was the varicella (chicken pox), because it is a live vaccine. So now I have chicken pox scars on my legs from childhood, but my body says that I never had chicken pox. More medical bizarreness! Even with a flu vaccine, I have to get the shot and not the mist. Sometimes this is a pain especially for my family. Bill has deployed, so he has needed a series of vaccinations and he always has to get the injections, otherwise he wouldn't be allowed to be around me. I hated anytime my illness caused a problem for someone else. Bill never complained. Sometimes he would tease me and say that he had to get the painful vaccination because of me and I have been known to tell him to suck it up. It's all in jest, but I wish he never had to think about it at all.

The day had come when I had finally completed all my vaccinations and I proudly proclaimed loudly at the doctor's office, "I'm a big girl now." There were a few nurses in the room, during my announcement and they started laughing and cheering. I had gotten to know many of them quite well over the years. I knew how many children they had and their favorite brand of make-up or shoes, many small tidbits about their lives. I loved it. They had become like a second family to me. They witnessed me going through the worse time of my life and they were all a huge support. Not only the nurses, also the entire staff at that time. If any of you are reading this, please know how grateful I am to each and every one of you! I would be remiss if I didn't mention Rosie, who was my nurse on my very first visit to the oncologist and she was also my nurse on my last appointment with Dr. Friend. She made me feel comfortable and if I was concerned about something, she knew how to get me to relax. Rosie was my one constant at my Connecticut oncologist and may God bless her and her family.

The years that have followed haven't been without a few bumps in the road. I found a new General Practitioner and her name is Dr Jen. I like her because she listens. You see, I became accustomed to oncologists who are a breed all their own. Even when the situation may be urgent, an oncologist, or at least all of mine, had special warmth about them. They believed me when I would suggest something or ask questions. I never felt rushed or dismissed. I supposed oncologists are unique in dealing with their patients, because they are all teetering in the unknown and the ever-changing science of the "c" word medicine. Whatever the reason, I am appreciative for the doctors who have crossed my path in this journey. I really dislike the whole "journey" catch phrase, but it fits here.

Anyway, Dr Jen pays attention. I know it's hard sometimes for doctors to treat bone marrow transplant recipients. It's still a fairly new procedure and the medical profession is just now learning the long-term effects of obliterating an ill immune system and replacing it with a healthy one. There's also the dilemma of how many of us really make it through this medical miracle. I've mentioned the variables of the patients before so I can only imagine how diverse our long-term effects may be. I feel like every time I see a new medical professional, I have to give a mini bone marrow transplant symposium. Don't get me wrong; I love being "that" survivor who is able to talk openly about the transplant process. I only wish that there were a better way to get all the information out to the medical community, because I know they are interested.

Chapter 37
The Five Year 5k

The next few years were a string of adaptations. I wanted to do something big for my five-year bone marrow birthday/anniversary, so I decided to do a 5k. Dr Friend said to go for it, and Dr Jen said a couple things needed to be checked out first. I had to go to see my orthopedist because I had been having issues with my left hip on and off. The orthopedist wasn't thrilled with my idea, because he had already operated on one knee years ago and I had been in and out of physical therapy for my hip, he wasn't sure that my body could take it. I was convinced that I could do it even though I had never been a runner. I had also read about other transplant survivors who had run marathons. I began my training in April of 2012. I couldn't even walk around the block when I began.

I came up with the bright idea of writing a blog about my training for the 5K. There was more to learn about running than I had ever imagined. I thought you put on some running shoes, some comfy clothes and you are off and running. No, that's not how it works. My orthopedist sent me to special running shoe store to be measured and to make sure I got the right size shoes to protect my knees and feet. I also learned specific exercises to strengthen my hips and how to stretch out my legs. I was amazed at how much stuff goes into running and protecting your body along the way. Then it was time to go sports bra shopping. Any dude reading this can just skip over the next paragraph, because there is a distinct possibility that you may be scarred for life.

Here's the deal. I happen to be one of those women with an ample bosom. Regular sporting good stores do not carry sports bras for the very well endowed, which doesn't make much sense to me at all. Those of us who tend to be big boned are the ones who should be working out and yet the sportswear industry makes it difficult to acquire the proper garments. Case in point: Lee and I went to our local sports store and I picked up the largest size sports bras that I could find to try on. While I was in the dressing room, I realized that the largest size bra had to go over my head. I was able to get one arm through and then the other and then over my head then..... the damn bra was stuck. It was stuck right under my neckline and my boobs were seriously bulging from under all the pressure of this torture device. I couldn't get it down any further and then the worst thing of all happened. I couldn't get out of the friggin thing. I was sweating profusely, which only made matters worse and panic was setting in. I contemplated putting my jean jacket on over the bubbling effect, to get Lee, who was waiting outside the dressing room, and have him help me get out of this boob apparatus. I was furious, I was upset and I was embarrassed. I stood there for a couple minutes in pain and somehow I calmed down enough to get one arm through, then the other and then I was free. I got dressed, stepped out of the dressing room and with tears in my eyes, I told Lee that I just wanted to leave. Once I was able to find appropriate bras online, I actually found the whole scenario in the store to be quite amusing. I thought if I didn't find a sports bra soon and I started running, I would be tucking my boobs into my waistband.

The day arrived to begin my walk/run days. I would walk for a certain amount of time and then run for a certain amount of time and the running increased, as I got further into training. I also began to emit this odor, which I had never quite noticed before. It was even worse than the chemo stench. I knew at that point that the flowery, fruity deodorants I had been using were not going to cut it anymore. My running shirts had taken on a life all of their own and I didn't think that they would ever smell clean again. It was time to bring out the big guns, men's deodorant. I didn't care if I smelled like an old man or musk or that sport scent, just as long as I didn't smell like body odor any longer. I found a men's sport gel that did the trick. PHEW!! I swear, even the bugs stayed away from me when I smelled like I had been living in a trashcan. Maybe that was why the neighbors went further into their yards as they saw me approaching. They wanted to be upwind.

Training took a toll on my body. I was getting sick often with bronchitis and it was difficult to keep the cough under control. I was determined to do the 5k even though I had to take breaks from training to recover from illnesses. I also suffered from shin splints and it sucked. I actually really enjoyed running, I only wished that my body enjoyed it as much as I did. The 5k was a fundraiser for the Leukemia and Lymphoma Society and I wasn't about to give up. I had put the shake down for money on too many of my friends and family not to see this thing to the end. One week before the race, I completed my first 3.1 miles in my neighborhood and I stood in the street and sobbed. I couldn't believe that I had come that far. Bone marrow to bone aching!

I didn't sleep at all the night before the race. I drove an hour to the beach where the race was taking place and I was nervous and excited. The only bad thing was, that Lee and Billy weren't there. There was a pre-deployment meeting for families and soldiers and they needed to be there. I offered to cancel the race, but Bill insisted that I do it. I had mixed feelings that day, because I really wanted to be with them. The atmosphere at the race was incredible. The running community is some of the friendliest, most helpful, encouraging people that I have ever met. I have to admit that I was overwhelmed by the amount of people. I always ran alone, so this was different and intimidating.

LLS made sure that someone was with me through the race just in case I needed something. I appreciated the company. It was a rough race for me. I was having issues with my hip and back cramping up the whole time. This was something that I have struggled with since the transplant, but this day it was exceptionally bad. It was difficult to even walk. The person who was with me asked me if I had even trained. I tried to explain what was going on, but I don't think she believed me. The fact that she asked me that, made me feel terrible. I did train, really I did!!!! Then in the last quarter mile, I developed a blister on the ball of my foot. It hurt and I was concerned about it getting infected, but I kept going. I thought, "Fuck this, I'm going to finish this race even if I have to crawl over the finish line!" I didn't crawl over the finish line, I ran over the finish line!! The band had already left; I'm sure they thought everyone had completed the race, but my friend from LLS, Kristen, was standing there cheering me on!! When I found out later that night that I was last in the race, I was pissed. Bill proceeded to yell at me and tell me, "What the heck, most people couldn't even run a 5k and would give up and you're a leukemia survivor, so stop it!!" Now my own son was putting my accomplishment into perspective. By the way, I raised over one thousand dollars for LLS in the process.

After the race, I began running (not in a race) high fevers, so my doctors put an end to my running. My body didn't appreciate that form of exercise. It took me a while to recovery from the whole thing, but I'm glad that I challenged myself. Exercise is still a complication for me. I've tried many different things along the way, but the cramping is brutal and my hip doesn't like to cooperate. Even after all these years, I'm still adjusting to what some may call limitations. I prefer to think of them as things that are making me explore other avenues and sometimes more exciting avenues. I may have never written this book if I was able to be as active as I used to be.

There was no way that Lee would let the five-year mark happen without a celebration. Lee wanted to give me a party, but I didn't want a big formal thing, so we opted for a party at the pub around the corner from our house. We had gotten to know the owner through a mutual friend and he was happy to have the party there. We invited the usual cast of characters. We had the pub menu and kept a tab at the bar for our drinking friends. The amazing thing that night was that one of Lee's old co-workers and his brother were the entertainment that night and they sang a song for me! I felt like the whole bar was there for me. Of course they weren't, but it felt that way. When Lee went to pay the bill for the festivities, we were shocked. It seemed that one of my friends had picked up the bar bill!! We don't know who paid the bill, but it was a pleasant and I suspect costly surprise. My friends are not big water drinkers, if you know what I mean. The next celebration will be at year ten!!

Chapter 38
Time Marches On

January 2014 was the time that my appendix decided it didn't care for my body any longer. I was frightened and angry. I was so afraid of having to spend time in another hospital; I put off going to the emergency room and waited for Dr Jen's office to open Monday morning. The attack started Sunday morning and waiting probably wasn't the smartest move I've ever made. Instead of getting checked out, Lee and I went living room furniture shopping. Yes, we were already looking for a new couch and chair because our husky Nikki had a pee pee leakage problem. I wasn't in a ton of pain and I kept trying to convince myself that I was only constipated, even though that never happens to me. I did feel a sharp pain on my right side while I was getting dressed and I did comment to Lee that I suspected that I had a problem, but I didn't want it to be true. Denial is a very powerful tool.

I knew something was up when I couldn't even eat dinner that night. With me, when I lose my appetite, we definitely know that something is amiss. Then I tried to sleep that night and the discomfort kept me awake. I called the doctor's office first thing in the morning. They couldn't fit me in until 2:00PM. Yikes! Needless to say, by the time I got there I was feeling crappy. The doctor examined me and said it was either my appendix or diverticulitis and I needed a CAT scan. I was sent home with a disgusting liquid to drink and Lee and I went to the next doctor for the scan. Yup, it was my appendix and I was sent directly to the emergency room with a computer disc of my results. Okay, here's the deal. I detest emergency rooms. They are nothing but a giant petri dish filled with nasty germs and horrible bacteria. Again, I cried when we walked in the door of the ER and Lee told them they needed to get me in a room. I'm really not a baby, I don't cry all the time even though it may seem that way. There were many people coughing and sneezing in the waiting room. I stood near the door to get fresh air and not breath in all their grossness from unknown illnesses.

I was called into triage fairly quickly and we were surprised that I didn't have a fever. I was relieved when I was given a bed. Until I realized, that it wasn't going in a room, ooohhh noooo, I was staying in hallway G. That's right, I was stuck in a hallway for hours. Then, as if that wasn't enough, the male nurse tried to put an IV in my arm as people passed and were hitting his arm. I was getting aggravated. Finally, someone came and protected the nurse from being bumped into and the IV was in, which meant that I could receive painkillers. Phew!! No sooner did they administer the painkillers and then they started asking me more questions. Seriously? There was literally a haze around everything I looked at and I'm fairly sure that I wasn't coherent for a short time. The pre-surgeon guy came up to me to ask me even more questions and the pain kicked in to the point where I couldn't speak and that was with drugs. I was only able to hold up my finger. No, not my middle finger, my hold on a minute pointer finger, even though my middle finger was an option.

The ER doctor, who looked like he had been working way too many hours, had been stopping by occasionally to check on me. There was one time that he came and sat on the gurney with me. The computers were down in the ER and he had to do all the paperwork by hand. He started asking me questions about the transplant. He was so interested in my story and the whole thing from a medical perspective. As a matter of fact, he called a specialist to make sure that the painkiller and antibiotic he was going to give me was okay because of all my allergies along with my sister's allergies. I appreciated his extra caution with my health. Then, the surgeon appeared. After he heard my medical history, he moved me to the top of the surgery schedule. He didn't want to take any chances of that blasted appendix bursting and causing an infection that I may not have been able to conquer. The surgeon also told me that I would be released from the hospital that night. That news made me feel one hundred percent better. What a relief! That was my number one concern. I desperately didn't want to stay in the hospital.

The surgery was a piece of cake. When I was in recovery, the nurse asked me if I needed any pain meds and I said, "No thanks, the pain is all gone," and it was. I had given Lee my sisters' cell phone numbers so he could let them know how the surgery went and his text to them said, "It's a boy!" He's a nut! They both appreciated the humor and were laughing when they told me about it. I was released from the hospital at one-thirty in the morning and we went directly to the all night pharmacy to get my medications. While Lee was inside the drug store, I called Bill because even though he didn't say so, I think he was concerned. I made sure that I texted Bill throughout the entire process. He had been through enough with all of my health issues, so it was important that he always knew that I was doing okay. I was up and about once all the darn medications were out of my system. Sometimes medicine is incredible.

Sometimes medicine is annoying. A couple years ago, Dr Friend's office and many doctors' offices went through a change. They became a part of what I call a conglomerate. When I would go there for my appointments every three months, something was always different. One time I went to my appointment and the office was moved to somewhere else in the hospital. I was pissed that I wasn't informed of the move, but one of the nurses told me that it was temporary until the old offices were re-done. Then, I looked around and realized that most of the nurses and office staff were different. For some people this might not have been a big deal, but to me it was monumental! I was extremely upset when I left that appointment. The majority of the people I had become so accustomed to were gone. I didn't like these changes one bit!! They were disrupting my routine. I didn't know or trust these people. They hadn't witnessed what I had gone through, they didn't know what to ask me, they didn't know what time of day I liked my appointments, they didn't know me. Grrr!

When Dr Friend's office finally moved back to the old location, it sucked. No longer was I able to get in and out of an appointment, nooooo, I waited about an hour a couple times. One time I was called into the office in a timely fashion, only to sit in, what I call a chemo chair, for quite a while. Again, my blood was boiling. Here's the deal. If you aren't getting chemo or a transfusion you never, and I mean never want to sit in one of those chairs. It messed with my head. I did everything in my power to pretend I was somewhere else, but I was so upset that I almost walked out. Briefly after my altercation with the chair, a survey was sent to my house about my experience with the new office. There was an option to be anonymous, but NO! I wanted them to know who I was and why I was pissed. I stressed that this had absolutely nothing to do with my doctor that I adore; it was only about the business of medicine. The business that forgets about the individual patient and how things are affecting them just to make more money, it makes me sicker than chemo did. I did receive a phone call from a woman who tried to smooth things over, just like she is supposed to do, but I still feel like they either didn't get what I was saying or that they didn't care. Either way it was wasted breath. I actually contemplated leaving the office, but I still needed Dr Friend.

Chapter 39
My Advice

There have been times that I've needed to look through the papers from the Boston hospital to refresh my memory from the almost 5 week long stay. Chemo brain is a real thing and when I say things get fuzzy or memories are nonexistent, I mean it. That's what made this process so difficult and cathartic. There were things I never wanted to recall again and yet here I was dredging the whole horrible experience back up and dealing with the after affects. There have been times that I actually felt like I was right back in the hospital, reliving the whole sordid thing. I wasn't in my living room any longer. I was closed away in my sterile, filtered air room. It was surreal and terrifying! This all occurred because I read about the hand tremors I suffered from for a short time. I had no conscience memory of the tremors until I read about them and then everything came rushing back. All the feelings from all those years ago were happening again. No time had passed. I was in my hospital garb, bald and I could almost see the sheet on the wall that had my numbers from the day written down. It sucked! I finally came out of it, but the memories remained and affected me for a while. So, anyone who is going through a life threatening illness…. GET COUNSELING! I fell through the cracks, so speak up and don't be stubborn. It doesn't make you weak to get counseling, it makes you smart. Tell your caregivers that it will be a good idea if they talk to someone also. This shit is no joke!

The most shocking flashback happened when I was in South Carolina for my niece's wedding. I went alone to the wedding, so I had a hotel room to myself. I proceeded to unpack and I was going to put my shampoo and soap in the shower. The bathroom had a tub and a stall shower. I thought it was good that there was a stall shower; it's easier than getting in and out of a tub. I reached into the shower and there I was back in Boston in the stall shower in my room. It hit me like a ton of bricks! There was no warning of this one. I wasn't in a medical environment. No reason for this shit to be happening again and yet it did. Now, I was pissed so I forced myself to take a shower in that stall shower twice a day for my three-day trip. I did it despite the life altering sucky memories. This was not going to defeat me. Leukemia had taken enough of my life, it wasn't taking anymore. I'm not sure if this was the best idea or how the professionals would deal with it, but it worked for me at the time. Having so many parts of my life being out of my control for so long, I felt like it was time for me to take control. So, I did! The funny thing is, I can talk to groups about being sick and the bone marrow process and I'm fine, but digging deep and being raw is a whole different story. I don't hide my feelings when I speak or maybe I kind of do. It's hard to let it go and it's hard to keep it in. There have been many other small occurrences, but these are the big ones. Hey, I may have many more along the way.

I'm sharing this because people always think that once you are in remission or your bone marrow is clear, that you are cured and all is well. Let me tell you, it's only the beginning. There are a million repercussions from having a serious illness that most people don't realize. Many people suffer from PTSD and any tragedy can bring back your worst nightmare. The treatment that has saved your life also changes your life. Some people suffer from infertility. Your eyesight and hearing can be in the crapper. Dry eyes, skin and mouth sores plague many people after various treatments. Constant fear of getting sick again and having a permanent script for anti-anxiety medication is common. Things that once were easy for you to do have now become difficult and exhausting. Muscle spasms can even make a trip to the dentist a chore. There may be a discomfort with traveling and the anxiety of a trip can overwhelm some people. Germs are a big one for me. I personally don't like to be in an enclosed area with a lot of people. The thought of a plane or train or a room packed with people can freak me out. When you know that you have a compromised immune system, those things can threaten your life and scare the poopy out of you. This isn't meant to be a "woe is me," I just want others who haven't been through something life threatening to understand where we may be coming from.

Sometimes, people like myself, don't want to admit the real reason why we can't do certain things because we all know that our friends and family are really friggin sick of hearing about our illnesses. Don't push too hard. Some reasons are physical and some are psychological, but all of it is valid. Don't tell us we just need to be grateful to be alive. I can say with much certainty that ninety-nine percent of us remember that every day without being told. Some days we are more grateful than others. We are doing our best with the cards we've been dealt and we need understanding without having to ask for it. Even when we do ask, certain people will always think we are using the illness as an excuse. We're not, but it's impossible to explain to some people.

There are many types of support groups on social media. I personally belong to two closed groups, one for AML and one for BMT survivors. They are wonderful tools that help us all feel like we aren't unusual or alone. One big thing about serious illnesses is that no one understands you like someone else who has gone through the same thing. It can be explained over and over again, but there really aren't any words to describe the feelings of pain and loss unless you've been there. The one thing that is constant is the way we all support each other. Every now and then there will be that one isolated asshole who acts like the know it all, but for the most part, the people are great. We get close to each other and emotionally invested in the triumphs and failures in the treatment of people we've never met. One morning I woke up to read that one of the young men I'd been following for months passed away. Yes, I cried and his death stayed with me for a while. It's never easy hearing about the death of one of your own, especially a young person. It reminds me that there is a responsibility in being a survivor. Why him and not me, runs through my mind more than I'd like to acknowledge. Every bit of suffering and every passing is a sucker punch. There are times I have to step away from reading the social media sights, for my own sanity. When you put yourself out there and get involved in "c" word organizations and social media sights, you also have to deal with more death than maybe you are prepared for. On the flip side, you also get more support and love than you are expecting. I guess it evens out. I just wish that my prayer list for those who have lost their lives wasn't so long. May our Lord bless each and every one of them and their loved ones.

Chapter 40
Now

Dr Friend retired from the oncology practice and he released me from their care, so now I only see Dr Jen for my blood work. I purchased a pen for Dr Friend before he left and I had the words "Hi Friend" engraved on it. We both got a little teary when we said goodbye and I miss seeing him. I did call him on my eight-year bone marrow birthday/anniversary to say hi and thank you. Boy do those words seem extremely insufficient!! I recently heard that Dr EA was going into research and leaving the hospital. I actually haven't seen him since the bone marrow reunion in Boston about five years ago. It was weird at the reunion, because I didn't want to leave. As many difficult memories that I have of being there, I also have some incredible wonderful memories of the Boston hospital. All these people who were strangers and held my life in their hands have become a part of my being.

Bill did deploy to a far away land and he returned to me safe and sound. The day he left on the plane was literally the worst day of my life. Even worse than the day I was told that I had the "c" word. I am so grateful that I get to tell him at least once a day that I love him and I am unbelievably proud of his bravery and his dedication to our country. Lee still works for the State and loves our two huskies. He also purchased a motorcycle and with all he went through with me, he deserved something special. Oh and he also purchased a boat. Wait a minute, he might be getting carried away.

Both of my sisters, Mel and Marlene are doing well. Mel's husband, Jack passed away in 2013 and it has been rough. Her heart is absolutely broken. Jack brought an amazing amount of laughter to an otherwise gloomy experience. Jack had no filter in his humor, which made him even funnier. I will remember his antics and smile every time I think of him. Our lives aren't the same without him. There is some good news on the horizon for Mel, she is going to be a grandma in a few months and we are all excited about our new addition. Marlene moved down south and she recently had her knee replaced. Marlene is a trooper and she joked her way through most of the pain. I will forever be grateful for their support and love through my trials and tribulations. I feel indebted to both of them. Sometimes it's difficult for me to constantly feel like I owe Mel for selflessly donating her bone marrow. I have often kept my mouth shut when something has bothered me because I don't feel like I have the right to say anything anymore. It's difficult. Please don't get me wrong, I love both of my sisters with all my heart and my gratitude is unwavering, it's just a debt that's always there.

Carol, my sister-in-law, passed away at the age of sixty-five. It was sudden and the entire family has been going through the shock and sadness of her passing. Carol was very simply one of the kindest and most thoughtful people I have ever met. Losing Carol has made me reflect on my own life. Carol always took the time to remember everyone's birthday and I mean everyone including cousins, friends and family. Her thoughtfulness was rare and far-reaching. I can't help but wonder about death at this time. Do we choose our own destiny before we are born? Are we taken from this earth when we have accomplished our souls purpose? Do we come back to this world to correct our wrongs and is that what an old soul is? Do we just die randomly? Are we here to teach other people some kind of life lesson or could it be all of the above? We can all believe different things about death and our beliefs can be strong and true to us, but the reality is, we don't know anything. That's what makes death so scary. We won't really know the truth about dying until we are there ourselves.

My life now isn't what it used to be, but neither is anyone else's. I left politics after serving for ten years. I chose not to run again. I felt like things were becoming too negative and I fought too hard to survive, to put up with all the bullcrap. I wasn't happy on the Council anymore, so rather than be one of those people who hangs on longer than they should, I decided to leave on my own terms. The best part of the decision is that my blood pressure is much better. The worst part of the decision is that I don't see the people I considered my friends anymore. I guess that is just one of those things that happen any time you leave a job or committee or any kind of group. It's sad, but true.

In 2008, I started an event called the "Walk of Honor." It starts out with a small ceremony and a mile walk, representing walking a mile in a soldier's shoes. It's a time to reflect and show our appreciation for the sacrifices of our military. In 2012, I added the "Warrior Award," which is given out to a Veteran who is the epitome of a warrior. Even though, in my opinion, anyone who is willing to put on a uniform is a hero in my eyes. In 2013, Lee came up with the idea to put commemorative bricks for Veterans along the walkway at the War Memorial. It has been a lot of work, but the reward of observing a Veteran seeing their brick for the first time has touched our hearts beyond belief. We found out that many families came from around the country to the dedication of the "Veterans Walkway" and some even planned parties celebrating their Veterans. I'm sure that I can speak for both Lee and myself when I say it was awe-inspiring to see the pride on so many Veterans faces. They should be proud and we should be proud of them too. The newest addition has been the granite pillars that line the walkway. Lee put a lot of blood, sweat and bruises into that project. A small ceremony that began all those years ago has taken on a life of its own. I'm not sure what is next in our Veteran work, but it should be interesting.

I recently spoke at the State Capitol on Rare Disease Day. MDS is considered a rare disease. I told my story, but my main objective was to get the point across that we need to raise awareness about these diseases. Too many times people aren't properly diagnosed, because there is such little knowledge in the medical community. Any patient with a rare disease really needs to be his or her own advocate. Sometimes, we need to teach our doctors. Some physicians are very receptive and some...not so much. I've had doctors tell me that a certain condition has nothing to do with my transplant, but through investigation, I have found out that it definitely was due to the transplant. I'm not an expert, but I know my body.

Recently, I went to my yearly eye doctor appointment and I found out that there is an issue with my retina. When the doctor told me about my eye, I felt like I was sucker punched. He was the last doctor that I needed to see for all my yearly exams. My first appointment was to see my ob/gyn. That's a stressful appointment because last year I was called back in to do an additional mammography. Everything turned out okay, but the sheer panic until the appointment...the "c" word panic was horrible. I made it through the gyno, dentist and blood work appointments with flying colors, until the eye doctor.

Since finding out about my eye, I wasn't myself. I went through all those too familiar feelings that have become a companion, like my shadow. I looked at myself in the mirror and I said, "Oh my God, please no more!!!" I was begging. I don't want to be that person that shit just constantly happens to and yet I feel like that was exactly who I was. In between my sobs, all I could do was yell to an empty living room "When will this ever end, when will I get a break?" It felt like every time I think things are going good and I was getting my mojo back...BAM!!! I didn't understand. I see rotten people doing unspeakable things and they are healthy, why the heck was something else happening to me. Through my tears the one thing that echoed in my head was, I'm so tired of all this, I'm just tired. I tried watching TV, but I didn't see or hear a thing. I know I did laundry, but there was no real recollection of the chore. I made dinner, but all that was in my head was fog. I was tired of worrying. I cried that day like I hadn't in a very long time. I made all of the weird noises and funny faces that come along with heart wrenching sobs. This shit was getting old. Maybe, just maybe all that was happening so I could really feel all those feelings from being sick and not just voice them as a memory. This was happening to me. I couldn't wait to go to bed so I could cry myself to sleep. I don't like anyone to see me that way. I was tired of being strong; I was numb.

The issue with my eye ended up being a partially detached retina and it was fixed by laser surgery in five minutes. Thank goodness! The problem was and always is the fear of an underlying illness. Any bump in the road can cause me to panic. I was afraid that the small hemorrhage in my eye meant that my platelets were low, which could mean that the leukemia was back. I was sick to my stomach and that happens every time a health issue rears its ugly head. The fear of getting sick again can be debilitating at times. I wish it would go away, but the reality of the situation is that the fear will be with me forever. I need to learn how to keep it controlled. I need to make it my friend and not panic.

Chapter 41
Survival

One thing I try to remember on a daily basis is that as long as I'm breathing, I'm a survivor. People who are going through treatment are survivors, whether they look at themselves like that or not. It is not necessary to complete treatment to be a survivor. I guess most people are survivors of one thing or another. I think the important thing is how you choose to go through your struggles in this life. I've learned a lot about myself through my reflections. I've realized that sometimes I'm a badass and sometimes I'm a whiney baby. I've learned that I can endure more than I could have ever imagined and much more than I ever wanted to. I've learned that my faith is so deeply embedded in my being, that I never really let it go, even through my anger with God. I always knew my relationships with my family are beyond loving and this only solidified what I believed to be true. I recently read a one line prayer that speaks volumes: "Let me not die while I am still alive." Now those are words to live by!

I will continue to speak to any group who will listen to me and I'll even reiterate to those who are sick of my voice. I'll never forget the time my friend told a gentleman that I was sitting next to that I am a leukemia survivor and his reaction was, "PEOPLE

SURVIVE THAT?" Yes, yes we do survive that and more and more of us are surviving every day. Not only are we surviving, but also we are living very productive lives. Our lives may be different than before diagnosis, I mean whose life hasn't changed over the years? I'm not super woman so believe me I still, on occasion, get pissed about getting sick. I still live in fear with every doctor appointment. Any bump, bruise, lump, cough or shortness of breath can set me into a tailspin. My weight is a constant struggle because of my fatigue. Maybe, I've also become a little lazy and I've become too close to my friends in the box (TV). I'm just kidding…kind of. There are some things that I do believe: humor was a huge component in my recovery. Going through this with the best possible attitude worked for me. The white light breathing became my form of faith. My family and friends showed me an immense amount of love to draw on and I am where I'm supposed to be. I'm hoping whatever is next is FRIGGIN AMAZING!

The End
Or Not

Made in United States
North Haven, CT
03 September 2022

23639011R00130